How To **Plate, Polish and Chrome**

How To **Plate, Polish and Chrome**

Dennis Parks

MOTORBOOKS

First published in 2006 by Motorbooks, an imprint of MBI Publishing Company, Galtier Plaza, Suite 200, 380 Jackson Street, St. Paul, MN 55101-3885 USA

MBI Publishing Company titles are also available at discounts in bulk quantity for industrial or sales-promotional use. For details write to Special Sales Manager at MBI Publishing Company, Galtier Plaza, Suite 200, 380 Jackson Street, St. Paul, MN 55101-3885 USA

Library of Congress Cataloging-in-Publication Data

Parks, Dennis, 1959-
    How to plate, polish, and chrome / Dennis Parks.
       p. cm.
    ISBN-13: 978-0-7603-2672-5 (softbound)
    ISBN-10: 0-7603-2672-X (softbound)
    1. Automobiles--Painting--Amateurs' manuals. 2. Chromium-plating--Amateurs' manuals. 3. Automobiles--Cleaning--Amateurs' manuals. I. Title.
TL255.2.P356 2006
629.2'60288--dc22
                                    2006024855

Editors: Jennifer Johnson and Lee Klancher
Designer: Julie Vermeer

Printed in China

On the cover: This all-aluminum bike, *Aluminum OHL EVO*, built by Arlen Ness, features one of Ness' early overhead-cam motors. *Michael Lichter*

Inset: A variety of surface finishes can be found in this engine compartment. This beauty has everything from shiny red paint, cast aluminum on the intake manifold, chrome on the valve covers, and anodized hose ends on the braided hoses.

On the title pages: A little bit of chrome goes a long way, and a lot can be overwhelming. From the blower scoop all the way down to the exhaust headers, most everything on this engine is chromed. With this many components and a large number of them being ribbed surfaces that require more detailed prep work, sending this out to a commercial chrome shop would come with a hefty price tag.

On the back cover: Painting between the fins helps to detail an otherwise off-the-shelf polished air cleaner. Whenever you do this extra detailing, you need to be sure to scuff the surface to be painted and use the appropriate primer so that the paint adheres properly.

About the author:

Dennis W. Parks' book credits include *How To Build a Hot Rod Model A Ford* (2001), *How To Build a Hot Rod* (2003), *American Hot Rod: How To Build a Hot Rod with Boyd Coddington* (2005), and *How To Restore and Customize Auto Upholstery & Interiors* (2005).

Parks has nearly 200 published car features in *Hot Rod, Truckin', Rodder's Digest, Street Rod Action, Australia's Supercar, Custom Rodder, Rod & Custom, Super Chevy, Custom Classic Trucks,* and *American Rodder* magazines.

With a vast knowledge regarding modification, Parks' experience includes working as the general manager of Morfab Customs, a full-service hot rod shop. He lives in suburban St. Louis, Missouri.

CONTENTS

DEDICATION

To all of the friends I have made over the last 20 years in my pursuit of fame and fortune through pictures and writings of hot rods and Harleys.

FOREWORD

I have been painting hot rods and choppers for more than 50 years, so I am more concerned with the painted finish than plated and polished accessories. However, I do know that the choice of every finish on a project must be thought of as a complete package during the all-important planning process. And, this planning should be done early in the building process. Too many people start putting pieces together and get way ahead of themselves without any thoughts of how they actually plan to finish the various surfaces of a vast conglomeration of parts. Oftentimes they end up causing more work for themselves, or incurring more expense to have someone undo something that didn't need to be done in the first place.

How To Plate, Polish and Chrome is an informative book that has really good information for the novice, as well as the pro painters and craftsmen. The information in this book covers pretty much everything needed to finish a hot rod or a chopper, whether it is a painted surface or one that is polished and plated. I've read all of the books my friend Dennis has written and find them all very informative. His writing style makes it easy to grasp the concept of how to do this kind of work. When you start a project armed with the knowledge contained in a book such as this, you are already ahead of the game when it comes to obtaining the desired results in painting, plating, or polishing. You just have to practice the techniques that you read about in this book. I just wish books like this had been around when I was learning to paint . . .

Remember, patience is the key. Virtually all of the processes required for building a hot rod or chopper are pretty simple when you get to thinking about it, but you have to remember to take your time and think about what you are doing. If you don't get the results that you desire, don't be afraid to go back and redo it. It is much better to admit your shortcomings and gain knowledge and experience than to brag about less-than-perfect work and not try to improve upon it. The processes are simple, but you have to practice them to get the best and consistent results.

—Roger Ward

ACKNOWLEDGMENTS

Many thanks to Tim Kohl at Mayhem Custom Paint & Airbrush, Mike Boyle at Fat Catz Plating, Jeff Rowlins at Arch City Choppers, Donnie and Jack Karg at Karg's Hot Rod Service, and Steve Walters and Ron Leadford at C. R. Metal Products for allowing me to come into their shops to take photos and ask questions. Thanks also to Roger Ward and John Kimbrough for their willingness to share their wealth of information and knowledge.

—*Dennis W. Parks*

INTRODUCTION

Whether your choice of transportation has two wheels or four (or more), fabricating it and making everything work together is merely half of completing the buildup of a chopper or hot rod. It's what you do during the second half of the project that catches everyone's attention by having visual impact. If you can't get their attention, it doesn't matter what is beneath the paint, polish, and chrome. A trick suspension or engine may be the real star of the show, but if nobody notices, it simply doesn't matter.

This book is written to help you choose what finishes to use and and to tell you how to apply those finishes to your rolling artwork. Each piece of your chopper or hot rod, and the finish that you choose for it, provides additional opportunities for detailing, and therefore, personalization. Be it painted, polished, or plated, all of these finishes require a certain amount of prep work before the final finish is applied. Most of this can be done by someone in a home garage, provided they have some instruction and the correct tools.

Most likely, not everything on your set of wheels is going to be polished or plated, so an added bonus of this book is a thorough discussion of how to apply paint to your ride. This paint, whether a solid color or enhanced by multicolor graphics, will serve as a gateway for additional detailing of your chopper by using various methods of plating or polishing. Most, if not all, of these polishing and plating techniques can be done at home. So, whether your goal is to save some money or be able to say you did it yourself, when it comes to "finishing" your ride, this book is for you.

My goal for this book is to provide the proper instructions for applying the finishes needed to make your project really stand out. It will also give you a list of necessary equipment to get you on your way toward obtaining professional-quality results, and save you some money in the process.

I hope that with how-to photos and text that doesn't automatically assume you already know what I'm talking about, this book will be a valuable tool to you in your "finishing" projects.

—*Dennis W. Parks*

CHAPTER 1
CHOOSING A FINISH

Each and every component that goes into a vehicle provides the builder and/or owner with yet another opportunity to detail their ride to perfection and greatly personalize it at the same time. This attention to detail is what separates the award winners and magazine features from the rest of the pack. Prepping the surface, choosing and applying the finish, and then detailing it to absolute perfection are all part of creating that perfect mode of transportation.

Whether you are making the scene in Sturgis, Louisville, or some smaller event close to home, you want your ride to really stand out. With the popularity of choppers

This contemporary chopper is typical of many choppers being built today. Often the builder starts with an aftermarket frame and components, relying on the variety of finishes on the various pieces to set it apart from the rest. All of the welds on this chopper have been smoothed with body filler prior to receiving primer and paint. Polished aluminum wheels, along with chrome and stainless accessories throughout, complement the flawless red paint.

A variety of surface finishes can be found in this engine compartment. This beauty has everything from shiny red paint, cast aluminum on the intake manifold, chrome on the valve covers, and anodized hose ends on the braided hoses. The forward portion of the valve cover does provide an example of one of the bad things about chrome: it reflects whatever is around it. In this case, it is red paint from the hood, which is not all bad, but it is something to be aware of when planning what types of finishes to use.

and hot rods and their growing numbers, how do you make yours rise above all of the others? You need flawless fabrication finished with mind-boggling graphics, on top of creative paint, highlighted by just the right amount of polish and chrome. Visual impact is the key to getting someone's attention.

Selecting a Finish

One of the first decisions that you will need to make before finishing your project is which components should use color and which should be polished. Paint can be applied to most surfaces, while polished finishes on metal are sometimes limited by the material itself. That is, some metals such as aluminum and stainless steel can simply be polished to obtain a shiny finish, while others require chrome plating to yield that shiny finish that is so popular.

Although most paint will be shiny (as a result of meticulous surface prep and paint application), painting is an entirely different procedure from metal polishing or chrome plating. Of course, there are those airbrush artists who can spray paint that looks like chrome, but that is another topic altogether.

Most likely, at least a minimal amount of your ride will be polished. However, don't think for a moment that everything needs to be polished or chrome plated to look great. Even if money weren't a determining factor, chrome plating everything would be very boring. A good balance of painted and polished components will yield a more pleasing result, while the perfect balance will totally blow you away. Being of a subjective nature, it is difficult if not impossible to define or even give an example of, but you know it when you see it.

Note the smoothness of the joints in the frame. This is done by first grinding the welds and then smoothing them with plastic body filler. This close-up shot of the engine shows the use of chrome and polished aluminum to detail the various components. The airbrushed checkered flag on the oil tank helps to break up the red paint scheme.

While you are in the planning stages of painting and detailing, look at all of the choppers or hot rods you can to gain ideas. Go to shows and take photos of what you like, as well as the things you don't like. Look at the photos a week or a month later and see if what first caught your eye still looks good, or if maybe that detail that you didn't like at first might be just the right personalizing touch with just the right amount of tweaking. Magazine racks are full of titles with features from around the world that should provide plenty of ideas. MBI (www.motorbooks.com) has published several books that should evoke creativity, inspiration, and the desire to get your project finished and hit the highway on your freshly painted set of wheels.

Paint

In its simplest form, painting is getting the surface smooth and then applying pigment (paint) over the surface. The bulk of the items on your machine can be painted or powder coated in just about any color you choose. Notable exceptions of course are the tires, any rubber hoses or belts, and light lenses. Although a monochromatic paint scheme can look great, more and more vehicles are becoming rolling works of art as builders/painters are expanding their use of flames, artwork, and other graphics.

This book will give you the lowdown on molding the seams of a set of custom handlebars using body filler to achieve that one-piece look. Basic surface preparation techniques that separate the pros from the amateurs will be discussed, along with how to apply base coat and clear coat paints. This will provide a firm foundation for applying graphics, such as flames that are masked, or freehand graphics that are done with an airbrush. Whether you limit yourself to the basic painting and have someone else add the graphics that really personalize it or do it all yourself, this book will provide you with the information on how to do it. What you add is vision, some basic artistic talent, and creativity.

Paint can be applied in a single stage, base coat–then–clear coat, or a tri-coat configuration. Years ago, fabricators only had the choices of lacquer or enamel paint, but now acrylic enamels and acrylic urethanes are available. To confuse the painting process even more, paint is available in much more than just solid colors. Metallics, pearls, candies, and even colors that change from one color to another in different light are now available. Combine this multitude of available colors with a wild imagination, and there is no end to the creative possibilities.

Painting between the fins helps to detail an otherwise off-the-shelf polished air cleaner. Whenever you do this extra detailing, you need to be sure to scuff the surface to be painted and use the appropriate primer so that the paint adheres properly.

Powder Coating

Powder coating is another popular way to apply color. Powder coating will be discussed in more detail later in this book, but the basic theory is to clean the parts, spray dry powder on them, and then heat the parts so that the powder melts into a liquid state and flows all around the coated pieces. There is a little more to it than that, but nothing that can't be done by most anyone who might consider working on a hot rod or chopper in the first place. So, if you contemplate powder coating enough parts for yourself and/or friends to justify the expense, you can do powder coating yourself, rather than send it out. Unlike paint that may result in runs, drips, and sags, powder coating does not open the door to many common flaws made by beginners. As in any finishing procedure, proper surface preparation is the key to success.

When compared to paint, however, powder coating is limited somewhat—its method of application is the limiting factor, as the coating is baked onto the material that it covers. With the temperature being in excess of 400 degrees Fahrenheit, the material being coated has to be able to withstand the heat, something not all materials can do. Pieces made of fiberglass (bodies or fenders) or soft metals such as aluminum or brass (some carburetor parts) cannot endure such temperatures. Even with its disadvantages, powder coating has its place, especially when durability and ease of maintenance are important considerations. Common applications of powder coating are frames, gas tanks, and suspension components. These pieces are made of metal that can withstand the heat applied in the application process and are greatly protected by this particular type of coating. Even though powder used in powder coating is now being produced in several more colors than just a few short years ago, it will most likely never be available in as many colors as paint.

Sparkle

As good as paint or powder coating can look by itself, it will usually benefit from at least a small portion of sparkle, even if just as an accent. Many accessories such as wheels, headlights, taillights, and handlebars are available in some sort of polished finish for the simple reason that even the best paint job in the world needs a little bit of contrast in the way of chrome plating or polished metal to look its best.

Depending on the particular type of metal and its inherent properties for any given component, different methods of finishing will be required to make that metal sparkle. Some metals can be given a highly polished finish, while others will yield a finish that is more low key or dull—but when used in the right proportions and with the right colors it will look great. Not that you should paint or polish each and every part of your chopper with a different finish, but knowing which finishes are available and learning to think outside the box will help create a one-of-a-kind chopper, if that is what you desire to do. Isn't owning a chopper or hot rod an expression of freedom and creativity in the first place?

Polished

Aluminum and stainless steel are probably the two most common materials in the motorcycle/automotive world that benefit from polishing. At the risk of oversimplifying, I'll just say these materials are polished by rubbing them with abrasive material to eliminate any surface imperfections. Abrasives designed for this purpose are measured in thousands of grits per square inch, rather than tens or hundreds used in smoothing a high school wood shop project. Compared to polishing compound, 400-grit sandpaper seems incredibly rough. And just as when you were sanding that woodworking project, you use progressively finer material until the desired finish is obtained.

Chrome Plated

To a certain extent, chrome plating is much like a combination of painting and polishing. As in applying paint, the preparation of the surface has a lot to do with the final appearance. If shortcuts are taken during the preliminary steps, they will quickly show up in the final product. Adding a layer of chrome plating to an improperly prepared piece is not going to make it suddenly look perfect. However, polishing is really just cleaning and smoothing the metal. The surface needs to be cleaned and smoothed perfectly in

Whether you like it or not is for you to decide, but there is no denying that lots of time and effort went into finishing this chopper.

This is another example of chrome reflecting everything around it. This is not so much of a problem on a chopper or early hot rod with no hood, but becomes very apparent on later vehicles with inner fenders and hoods. One way to avoid this reflection problem is to use a satin finish on the plated items, or to use a flat or semigloss finish on the surrounding painted surfaces.

Black paint on this chopper is highlighted by a multitude of custom components that have been well polished. It is difficult to distinguish between chrome plating and polished aluminum or stainless, as either of them will provide plenty of sparkle if done properly.

order for the chrome plating to look right. And like paint, chrome plating applies a new, albeit thin, layer of material to the object being chrome plated.

Gloss or Satin

Whether the surface in question is going to be painted or polished, another question when determining its finish is whether it should be glossy or satin. This may be a question deemed more appropriate in automobiles, as satin finishes are more commonly used in underhood or interior applications. However, there are also a few situations on a chopper where something less than gloss might be ideal.

Gloss

Almost any surface that is going to be readily seen or that will need to be cleaned on a regular basis (admittedly most, but not all, portions of a chopper) will benefit from a smooth, glossy surface. Most paste wax products are not intended to be used on nonglossy surfaces or on surfaces that are rough or uneven. A smooth, glossy surface allows you to apply a paste wax to protect the finish from sun damage and rock chips, keeping the finish in good condition. Likewise, surfaces that are chrome plated or otherwise polished can be cleaned and protected with polishes made specifically for the type of material.

Satin

What are you *not* going to see on a chopper? The underneath side of the fenders should be an obvious example. These surfaces are subject to considerable abuse if you ride your chopper at all, so a not-so-glossy surface will hide some of the inevitable imperfections that will arise from road rash. Not that anyone is going to see the insides of the fenders, as there will not be much room between the tires and the fenders anyway.

This engine compartment looks much like an Ansel Adams photo, in that it features pure white, the blackest black, and several shades of gray in between. Although what has been painted and what has been powder coated is difficult to distinguish, there are several examples of each. A guess would be that the master cylinder, alternator, valve covers, and alternator brackets have been powder coated. The engine block and inner fenders have been painted, while the air cleaner and radiator cap are milled aluminum.

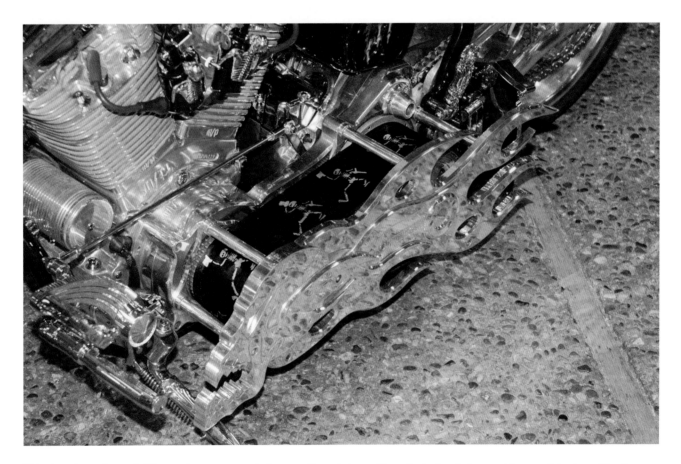

This shot shows the vast difference in appearance between satin and glossy. The cylinder heads have not been polished, resulting in a satin finish. The belt guard, on the other hand, has been polished extensively.

Plenty of glossy surfaces in this photo. The paint is base coat/clear coat, while the engine accessories are all polished and/or chrome plated.

Although it looks fine as is, this wheel sports its natural aluminum look, since it has not been polished. This is what the wheel would look like right off the factory milling machine.

They're not as flashy as chrome and polish, but many late-model Harleys feature lots of textured, flat-black surfaces on and around the engine—an area that is prone to rock chips and road rash. Perhaps this is more suited to a sport bike, but the first guy (or gal) to show up with this treatment on their chopper will be drawing a crowd . . . and won't be spending as much time polishing, either.

Another example of a satin finish, although perhaps more common on hot rods than bikes, is billet aluminum. Billet aluminum in its usual form after being machined is dull, but it can be polished. This makes it an interesting material to use if you are building either a chopper or a hot rod. If desired, you could prime the framework and accessorize with billet pieces to the point of getting your ride on the road. Then, when you take the time to detail it, you could apply finished paint and polish all of the billet aluminum pieces, giving your bike or rod a completely different look in the process.

Paint

Just like everything else, most finishes have different price tags, so it's not simply a decision of which you like best. If you are on a strict budget, you could paint everything . . . you could even simply coat everything in epoxy primer and forgo the actual paint if you are on a *really* strict budget. On the other hand, if money is no problem, you could have almost everything chrome plated, or perhaps even whittled out of billet aluminum. Chances are that you are somewhere in between these two extremes. If that is the case, you will need to decide which pieces to have painted and which ones should be polished.

Relative Costs

Although the price of a paint job can vary from pretty low (if a painter needs some money) to very high, paint is still on the lower end of the pricing spectrum. Several factors play a part in this.

First of all, a chopper doesn't require a lot of paint, as there simply isn't a whole lot of surface area to put it on. Depending on the mixing ratio of reducer to paint for whatever paint system you may be using, a pint of paint may be all that is needed for your chopper. Compare this to a typical hot rod that may require two gallons of color,

and it is easy to see that cost in materials alone will be much smaller.

Secondly, labor for prepping, priming, and painting a chopper is going to be minimal when compared to a hot rod or any other automobile. Except for the gas tank and the fenders, almost everything else on a chopper is tubular or flat plate. Sure, there are some nooks and crannies to prep, but there aren't that many of them and they don't require much work. The gas tank and fenders will take the bulk of the time, but even those are pretty easy to sand, prime, and paint.

If you are planning to paint a hot rod, you no doubt already realize that there are several more parts, and they are typically larger. To avoid becoming overwhelmed, take them one or two at a time.

This chopper is under construction, but still gives a great appearance in its raw form. With materials such as aluminum or stainless steel that don't rust, one could certainly build a badass chopper that doesn't have a bit of paint on it.

Polished aluminum wheels and chrome-plated fork tubes look great on the front of this chopper. The two polished surfaces have distinct differences in appearance, yet they look great together. Of course, either one of these will look fantastic when combined with red paint. Whether you really like red or not, it will always draw a crowd.

Do It Yourself

For the above reasons, a chopper is a relatively small project, so it is a better choice of projects for a beginner to tackle. A good place to start detailing your chopper or hot rod project is by molding in all of the seams on the frame. With all of the necessary welding completed and welds ground smooth, body filler is used to blend all of the edges together, making the frame look like it was all one piece from the very beginning. Shape the filler so that there are no sharp edges anywhere, and sand it until it's as smooth as a baby's behind. Spraying primer over this, and then sanding the rough spots that the primer brings out, will provide good experience. As long as the body filler is mixed thoroughly, and it and the primer applied properly, nothing you are doing can't be easily repaired if you don't get the shape quite right. The worst thing that can happen is that someone else will have to grind it all off and then razz you about it forever. Spraying paint can be a little tougher, as it requires a little more attention to

detail. You will need to be somewhat more precise with your air pressure and mixing ratios with paint, but that is not difficult. Due to its shape, a motorcycle gas tank is not the easiest of items to paint—neither are wheels. However, as long as you remember to keep the spray gun nozzle perpendicular to, and at the right distance from, the surface, even that will become simple with practice.

You will need specific equipment for your painting project, though. The tools you'll need will be discussed in more detail later in this book, but if you don't have them and plan to do paint work anyway, you will need to add the cost of this equipment (whether purchased or rented) into the cost of your paint job. As for the basics of achieving a professional-looking paint job, you will need a high-quality spray gun, an air compressor and air hose, and a respirator—at the very minimum. A decent spray gun capable of spraying automotive-type paint can be found easily for around $100, but can quickly go upward in price, depending on quality, adjustability of the spray pattern, and brand-name recognition. A new air compressor with enough volume and pressure for this kind of painting is going to start at around $400 to $500, with more volume and more pressure costing more. A respirator is cheap at around $20. So, for not much more than $600, you can have all of the essential equipment that you need. Obviously, the price of the paint, primer, sandpaper, and other expendable items will vary, depending on the particular job.

If you are just going to be painting your bike or automobile this one time and don't plan on doing any additional paint work, you could probably rent the necessary equipment, depending of course on the availability of tool rental centers in your particular locality. On the other hand, if you are considering doing this type of work on a regular basis, you should consider investing in higher-quality tools that will cost more at the onset, but will ultimately save you money in the long run.

Do You Have What It Takes?

Sure, you like riding your chopper or hot rod—why else would you own one? The question is, do you really want to learn to do the work involved with painting one? Do you

Although it typically has a satin (or as some people would say "dull") finish, brushed aluminum certainly has its place as an acceptable surface finish. It requires a little less effort to keep in presentable condition, so it is more suitable for choppers that are ridden often, as opposed to those that are strictly show bikes.

have a good eye for colors and a steady hand for applying artwork or handling a spray gun? Do you really want to sand that gas tank or fender until it feels like your arm is gonna fall off? I am assuming you do, and that is great—this book should help you get started toward applying a paint job that you can be proud of.

Enough Space

A chopper doesn't take up quite as much room as a hot rod when it is disassembled, but a significant amount of room is needed when finishing a complete chopper project. The frame will be the largest single object, but there will also be a pair of fenders and a gas tank that need to be painted. Unless you plan to paint them in separate sittings, they will have to be situated far enough apart that overspray from one part is not ending up on another part. You will also need room for storing the engine and tires so that they aren't coated with paint overspray or buffing compound.

Environmental Issues

Polishing metal is not going to send up any red flags to the environmentalists in your neighborhood, but you can bet that if a neighbor has it out for you already, they will notice when you are spraying any paint. Paint and its related products are much safer than they were years ago, if you follow all of the safety warnings and instructions regarding their use. Like anything in today's world, if used in accordance with the intended purposes and with some common sense, painting in your home garage is not going to hurt anything. Safety equipment and practices will be described in more detail in chapter 2.

Take it to a Professional

For those same reasons listed above (little material and not much labor involved) having your chopper painted professionally shouldn't be out of the question if, for whatever reason, you choose not to do it yourself. Conversely, a hot rod is more involved, making it more costly to have painted professionally. Although it will be more work, cost alone may be enough reason to do the work yourself.

Since a chopper is a relatively small project, many auto body shops take them in to use as filler jobs while they are

When machining custom pieces, such as this mirror and handlebar grip, you should design them so that they look like they match. Although the mirror is essentially a triangle, it still echoes the pattern that is milled into the handlebar grips, which are more of a diamond. Whether these pieces are highly polished aluminum or chrome plated is difficult to tell, but they are consistent in appearance.

waiting for replacement parts for collision jobs. With the high number of auto body shops in some areas and the competitive nature of the business, an auto body shop that is short on business might make you a good deal on painting your pride and joy.

If your profession does not provide you with enough spare time to get your chopper disassembled, painted, and reassembled in a couple months, having it painted professionally seems to make even more sense. Pay the money to have someone else do it while you are working, so that the chopper will be ready when you have the time to "head out on the highway lookin' for adventure."

Unless you make your living building hot rods or Harleys, nobody says that you have to build your own, and there is no shame in paying someone else to do it for you. And, if you do make your living building them, you probably realize that it still might be easier and quicker to pay someone else to build one for you. Not that you would want to patronize a competitor, but if you do high-quality work and charge a fair amount for the work you produce, you are probably going to be too busy to produce a frivolous toy for a nonpaying customer like yourself. Of course, chances are slim to none that you would actually have someone else build one for you, even if it means that your personal ride may never get finished due to business from paying customers.

Powder Coating

Although the process has been around for several years and is used extensively in manufacturing, powder coating for individual hobbyists is still in its infancy, making pricing anything but standardized. Much like anything else, the larger the piece to be coated, the more it costs at any one shop. But, rates from shop to shop can vary quite a bit, depending of course on factors such as how busy they are, how busy they want to be, and if they even want to work on your particular project.

Years ago, all powder coating was done for manufacturing companies that would have large runs of identical parts that would all be coated in the same color. One run of a thousand or so widgets that were being powder coated in gloss black would have to be completed before another run of anything in any different color could be done. If you happened to take your parts to the shop at the right time, and they would even consider doing work for individuals, and if you wanted your parts to be coated the same as whatever was being coated the next day, you could sometimes get your parts powder coated in a timely manner, but it would usually be expensive.

However, as powder coating is becoming more common, more shops are doing this work on a custom basis. While they may be taking the short-run jobs that are too small for the production shops, the basis of their work is for hot rodders and bikers. Other than a complete hot rod chassis or lengthy suspension components, most of the pieces for these hobbyists are relatively small and therefore do not require an extremely large curing oven, which is usually the overall determining factor for getting something powder coated.

Do It Yourself

Thanks to the offerings of many automotive restoration companies, powder coating can now be done in your home shop. The downside is that the cost of the equipment is considerably higher than that used for painting, especially if you are going to be coating large parts. If you are going to be powder coating several small parts that would fit inside a typical residential kitchen oven, the cost is not prohibitive. Do-it-yourself powder coating is essentially limited only by the size of the parts you choose to coat and the cost of an oven that is large enough for those parts.

A do-it-yourself quality powder-coating gun will cost less than $150, while a gun suitable for larger parts or small production runs will be around $750. In either case, you will need an air compressor or a large air tank with a regulator. For curing the powder, a discarded kitchen oven will do the trick for small parts and can be found for nearly nothing if you keep your eyes open. (NOTE: Once the oven has been used to cure powder coating, DO NOT use it for food preparation.) On the other hand, bench-top ovens large enough to cure pieces up to around 3 feet long sell for approximately $6,000, with larger ovens costing considerably more. An alternative to an oven that is fully enclosed is the use of infrared lamps. These can be found in many different sizes and prices.

Professionally

If you have large parts to be powder coated, such as an entire chopper frame or hot rod chassis, you will most likely be forced to find a professional powder coater who has an oven large enough for your particular project. Looking in your local telephone directory under "metal finishing" will provide some sources for professional powder coaters. Since some of the listings may be for large-run production companies and others for custom shops, simply asking other enthusiasts might be easier. Wherever people who share your interests may congregate, whether it is at a car or bike show, or a chat room on the Internet, this will be the best place to ask around for recommendations on finding someone to do the work you are looking to have done. Those who have had powder coating done for them will most likely be able to give you a good idea of the quality of the work and approximate prices, as well as contact info.

An advantage of having a professional do your powder coating is that he or she should possess a better working knowledge of powder coating characteristics. Materials used for powder coating can be varied to produce different finishes. Curing at different temperatures or for different lengths of time can also vary the characteristics of the final finish. A professional's experience and knowledge will most likely yield the desired finish for you on the first try, while your first attempt may not give you the results that you had envisioned, if you are using anything other than a standard color.

A little bit of chrome goes a long way, and a lot can be overwhelming. From the blower scoop all the way down to the exhaust headers, most everything on this engine is chromed. With this many components and a large number of them being ribbed surfaces that require more detailed prep work, sending this out to a commercial chrome shop would come with a hefty price tag.

Polishing

Polishing is one of those finishes that you will have a much better appreciation for after you have gone through the process of doing it yourself, as it is very labor intensive. For that very reason, the cost for this work can range from expensive to outrageous. All the more reason to learn how to do the work yourself.

Do It Yourself

Equipment used for polishing can range from a bench top- or pedestal-mounted buffer to a handheld buffer (which could be a buffing wheel attached to a die grinder or hand drill). A bench-mounted buffer will range from just a tad over $100 for an economy model to less than $600 for a very nice buffer. For polishing small parts, a flexible shaft that attaches to a drill motor can be had for less than $50, while the various shapes and sizes of buffing wheels that attach to it or to a die grinder are less than half that price.

The size of the parts you can polish and the time it takes to polish them pretty much depends upon the equipment you are using. If you have the necessary equipment already, polishing your parts is free, except for the buffing compound that you use in the process. The cost of the polishing compound is minimal when compared to the hourly rate at almost any shop, so polishing is the one finish that you should consider doing yourself if you are only going to do portions of the work on your wheeled project.

Since polishing is so labor intensive, sending parts out to a shop may result in a longer wait than you may anticipate. If it is the middle of the winter, this may not be a problem, but if you are getting ready to go to Sturgis or Louisville, you may not get your polished parts back in time. On the other hand, if you are doing the work, you can stay up half the night working on them if that's what it takes to get it done. You also have the option of saying that something is good enough for now, if need be. Not that any of us ever wants to settle for less than perfect, but if just being there is more important to you, you can make that decision. Of course, hearing everyone say that the polished pieces on your vehicle look fantastic, and then being able to say you did it yourself, will no doubt give you an ego boost.

Professionally

If you are polishing something that is relatively flat without intricate and complex shapes, such as front forks, wide rear fenders, or windshield frame, you can make do with a bench-mounted or handheld buffer for most of your buffing. However, if you are contemplating buffing and polishing something that has lots of crevices and tiny orifices, such as engine cylinder heads, highly detailed foot pegs or pedals, or other custom work, you will need smaller

attachments for reaching those areas. Anyone who does metal polishing professionally probably already has a wide variety of grinding discs, buffing wheels, and all of those neat gadgets for reaching into all of those difficult-to-reach spots. If you foresee doing lots of polishing in the future, it may be in your best interest to purchase all of the necessary accessories. But if you have no intention of polishing anything beyond this project, maybe you should let the pros do it. They will have everything needed to do the job correctly and may have the task completed before you can round up all of the necessary tools. Having a professional do the work can be expensive, but so is buying tools that you never use again.

Chrome Plating

Do It Yourself

Not long ago, having something chrome plated meant that you had to farm out the work, often shipping it halfway across the country. That is no longer the case, as several companies now sell kits for do-it-yourself chrome plating. The most common problem that hobbyists encounter is having plating tanks of adequate size. Small parts, such as most of those found on choppers or hot rod interiors, are not a problem. Having a tank large enough for an automobile bumper, however, is beyond the capabilities of most home plating shops.

Professionally

Because a chrome plater's reputation is on the line with each piece that leaves the shop, most platers would rather you not do any prep work. This is usually the case with painting also, but some painters will allow you to do the bodywork and priming, as they spray a coat of sealer between your work and theirs. It is in their best interest to control all of the preparation work to ensure that their plating looks absolutely top notch. Of course, they have to charge you for all of this labor-intensive work.

A SELECTION OF POPULAR FINISHES

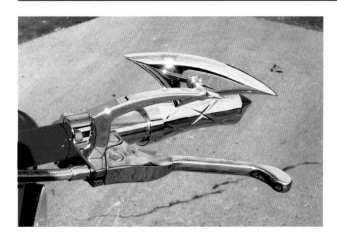

From the opposite side of the same mirror and handlebar grip, it is apparent that the top edge of the mirror and the mounting bracket have the same arc, again to provide consistency in appearance. The mirror also comes to a distinct point, just like the handgrip.

Powder coating is a good method of adding color to cylinder heads, but it must be done with extreme caution. Knowing exactly what material the heads are made of, its characteristics, and keeping a close eye on the temperature of the curing oven will go a long way toward completing this successfully—being a bit lax may even result in heads that are warped.

Semigloss black paint, brushed aluminum fork tubes, and thermal wrapped exhaust pipes provide a sinister look on this no-nonsense chopper. I'd be willing to bet that this one gets ridden often.

There is certainly nothing wrong with a solid base color highlighted by a set of contrasting color flames. Just be sure that the layout of the flames flows with the lines of the bike itself.

Bright white scallops do a great job of toning down an otherwise eye-searing orange paint job on this roadster. Orange paint is a great compromise between red and yellow. It has all of their benefits, yet orange can be a bit much for some people's tastes. The addition of these scallops doesn't distract from the car at all, and would be a good way to personalize a vehicle.

CHAPTER 2
TOOLS, MATERIALS, AND SAFETY

Before you can do any paint-related work, you need to have the right tools and the right materials—and you need to know how to use them safely. Having the coolest ride around doesn't do you any good if you can't see it or ride it. Improper painting techniques can cause you serious health problems.

Necessary Equipment

As with almost any task, the list of necessary equipment depends largely on whether you are going to be doing the job one time for yourself or if you are in the business and doing this type of work on a regular basis. If you are in the business, time is money, so your choices and priorities on tools will depend greatly on how much time they will save compared to their cost of ownership. The time saved will only be a critical factor if you are established sufficiently enough to have a waiting list, and therefore don't have the time to do the work in question by hand or with what you already have. On the other hand, if you are going to be working on just this one project with no intention of doing similar work again, you should steer clear of expensive tools that you most likely won't be using again.

Air Compressor

If you are going to be using any pneumatic tools, it should be obvious that you will need to rent, borrow, or purchase an air compressor. Good air compressors seem to be coming down in price and are available in a wide variety of shapes and sizes. They are also available in discount stores, building supply centers, and hardware stores, as well as at locations that sell automotive paint.

If you don't have an air compressor or are looking to upgrade with a new unit, determine the types of equipment

Whether you are cleaning metal with a media blaster or a grinder, or applying paint, a large-capacity air compressor is essential to using your time efficiently. Pneumatic tools aren't an absolute necessity for finishing metal, but their use really cuts down on the time and hard work needed to complete the task.

that you will be powering with this air compressor and make sure that it will suit your needs. If you are going to be using it for painting only, a 5- or 6-horsepower compressor will most likely be adequate. However, if you are looking to provide air for a commercial shop that will be using sanders, grinders, and spray guns simultaneously, you will need a larger compressor in the 10- to 15-horsepower range.

Volume

The volume or amount of air that a compressor can deliver is measured in two distinct, yet equally important, ways. One is a measure of the compressor itself and is measured in cubic feet per minute (cfm). Each piece of equipment that you plan to run with your air compressor requires a certain amount of air. This requirement is provided in the owner's manual of the pneumatic equipment. If you know that your new spray gun requires 12 cfm, but your old air compressor will only pump 9 cfm, you will need a new compressor, as well.

The other measurement of an air compressor is for the tank and is listed in gallons. If you are using a conventional, siphon-feed spray gun, a 5-horsepower compressor with a 20-gallon tank would be sufficient for spraying most automotive-grade paint materials. However, if you are using an HVLP spray gun, the 5-horsepower compressor might be sufficient, but you would quickly deplete the air from the small tank, causing the compressor to run almost constantly to keep up. For a one-time painting situation, you could get by with this smaller tank, but you would have to stop in the middle of spraying to allow the compressor to catch up. This would quickly become annoying on all but the smallest of parts.

Pressure

It is important to apply automotive paint at the pounds-per-square-inch (psi) rating that the paint manufacturer recommends. This information is indicated on the container label or in the product's application literature. Although the control gauge setting on the compressor may indicate 40 psi while in a static condition, the actual pressure while spraying paint may drop to 30 or 35 psi, depending greatly on the length of air hose and its inside diameter. For standard production paint guns, the air hose should be a minimum of 5/16 inch with a maximum length of 25 feet. For HVLP spray guns where higher volume is the key, a 3/8-inch minimum inside diameter hose, as well as hose ends, quick couplers, and connections to spray guns, should be used.

Dry Air

Any time the demand for air exceeds the supply, the air compressor must run. The more that a compressor works to maintain pressure, the hotter the air supply becomes. As the air inside the compressor gets warmer, moisture is created as the warmer air begins to cool off while moving through the air supply lines and air hoses. When present, this moisture can play havoc with your paint application. An inline drier/filter will minimize the moisture that reaches your spray gun, but eliminating or at least minimizing the formulation of moisture in the air system in the first place is a better tactic.

Paint Guns

Various brands of paint spray guns are available with Sata, Sharpe, and DeVilbiss being three of the most popular for automotive or motorcycle refinishing. Regardless of the brand, two different types of spray guns are available. A standard production gun is the largest and usually features a 1-quart-capacity cup. A smaller spray gun, referred to as a detail gun, features a 6- or 8-ounce-capacity cup and a

Shown is a Sharpe filter/drier/regulator. A copper hard line supplies air from the compressor. The compressed air then passes through the filter/drier to eliminate moisture or other contaminants, and then can exit from either of two regulated outlets.

27

These two spray guns have served the author well for several years, especially for spraying primer. The larger one is a conventional siphon feed gun with a 1-quart cup. It can apply lots of material in a short time over a large area, such as a fender. The smaller gun is a touchup or detail gun, depending on whom you talk to. It has a much smaller cup capacity, but will get into smaller areas that a full-sized gun can't. Both require a lot of air pressure, which results in lots of overspray.

trigger assembly located on top of the gun instead of the handle grip trigger found on a typical production gun.

Most wholesale or retail outlets that sell automotive finishing products also sell spray paint guns and their related accessories. For a production spray gun, prices start at around $60 and go upward, depending on the brand and precision quality. A detail gun will cost slightly less, but will rise in price accordingly just as a production gun does.

Spray guns are available for sale at many locations, although most professional painters will suggest buying a paint spray gun from the same dealer who sells paint. Although the price may be slightly higher, having a knowledgeable salesperson might very well be worth the extra money. It is a known fact among professional painters and paint retailers that product literature may suggest a particular setting for inlet air pressure, while actual experience can

assure you that a higher inlet air pressure is necessary for the desired results. Without this firsthand experience, your brand-new spray gun (at whatever price range) may never work as well as desired. For HVLP spray guns, this inlet air pressure is even more critical than conventional spray guns of the past.

Conventional

Conventional spray guns, long the norm, are quickly losing favor. They typically require air pressure of 60 psi or more, depending on the material being sprayed. This high pressure propels the paint at the surface with such force that approximately 65 percent of the material actually goes up in overspray—ending up in the air or on the floor, rather than on the surface being painted. Higher pressure is also more likely to stir up existing dust and dirt that will eventually fall into fresh paint.

High Volume, Low Pressure (HVLP)

With growing concern over atmospheric pollution, government agencies, civic organizations, paint manufacturers, paint equipment companies, and painters have all been forced to look for ways to minimize paint-related pollution problems. Paint manufacturers have reduced the amount of volatile organic compounds (VOCs) in paint products by developing new formulas. VOCs are the portions of paint or paint products that evaporate into the atmosphere. The solvents (thinners and reducers) that keep paint in a liquid state are the main cause of paint-related air pollution. Any gallon of paint may include up to 90 percent solvent, while thinners and reducers are 100 percent solvent.

Even though the paint manufacturers have done their part to minimize the VOCs in their products, they cannot be removed completely. The application process still releases the VOCs to the atmosphere. A viable way for the end user to minimize the release of VOCs is with the use of high volume, low pressure (HVLP) spray paint systems.

When HVLP systems were introduced, they were composed of a spray paint gun and a turbine system, rather than a conventional air compressor. This new HVLP concept made good sense and was widely accepted as a good idea, although the actual process gave less than desired results. The problem was that the turbine system used to propel the paint caused the air to get too hot, causing the paint to dry too quickly, sometimes even before it reached the intended surface. Although the original turbine systems have been redesigned, a more practical solution is the development of HVLP spray guns that operate with a conventional air compressor. This is good news for anyone, but especially for anyone who is just beginning to equip their shop, as an air compressor is much more versatile than an HVLP turbine paint system.

With an HVLP spray gun, a higher volume of paint can pass through the ports and nozzle at a lower pressure. Since less pressure is being used, more paint material actually adheres to the surface, rather than bouncing off when propelled at the higher air pressure. This accounts for an approximate reduction in overspray waste by 50 percent. Less waste also means that less paint material is actually needed for the job, thereby reducing the cost of materials. With the cost of paint products being what it is, spending a little more for an HVLP spray gun will quickly pay for itself. Plus, cruising in clean air has to be more fun than in polluted air.

Although the paint material is coming out of the nozzle of an HVLP spray gun at low pressure (approximately 10 psi), the gun itself will still require approximately 60 psi to achieve the suggested spray tip pressure. This is important to remember when choosing an air compressor.

Siphon Feed

In addition to conventional or HVLP, spray guns can be further classified as siphon feed or gravity feed. On either a production gun or a detail gun, the paint cup of a siphon feed gun is located below the air nozzle. More air pressure is necessary to siphon the paint material out of the paint cup. This higher air pressure causes approximately 75 percent of the paint material to end up as overspray on a non-HVLP siphon-feed spray gun.

This is a conventional siphon feed spray gun, and the HVLP gun that replaced it for spraying color in the author's shop. Notice that the HVLP gun has the paint cup mounted above the air nozzle. In addition to using gravity to assist the paint flow, this gun seems to be more balanced in regard to weight. That may not seem like a big deal, but if you do a lot of spraying, it will make a difference in how your arm feels at the end of the day. The HVLP gun also requires a pressure regulator and gauge at the air inlet to easily adjust the air to provide the best air pressure at the gun tip.

Gravity Feed

Unlike a siphon-feed spray gun, the paint cup for a gravity feed gun is located above the air nozzle. Slightly less air pressure is needed, as gravity does part of the work to feed the paint into the nozzle. However, on a non-HVLP spray gun, this will still result in approximately 65 percent of the material being wasted as overspray.

Production Gun

For painting large easily accessible panels, such as fenders or custom sheet metal, a production spray gun works well. Typically having a 1-quart paint cup, a fair amount of material can be sprayed before the need to refill.

Detail (Touchup) Gun

A detail gun is especially suited for smaller areas, touchups, or anywhere that simply isn't accessible with a large production gun. With the trigger mounted on the top of the gun and operated by the full length of the user's index finger, maximum control is achievable, even in confined areas.

A detail gun is also used to apply relatively large amounts of paint, such as a background to a mural or other artwork that will be completed with an airbrush.

Airbrush

Smallest of small, an airbrush is what is used for almost all freehand artwork, intricate stenciled or masked art, or anything else that is simply too small for a production or detail spray gun. The paint cup is extremely small, so an airbrush is necessarily limited to applying very small amounts of paint at any one time.

Paint Gun Maintenance

Like any piece of precision equipment, spray guns need consistent cleaning and maintenance. The cleaning isn't difficult to do, but it must be done after each use. With the very small size of passageways for both air and materials, any clog can be fatal to a spray gun. Primer, paint, clear, or any other material that is allowed to dry in the gun will be difficult to remove.

Whenever you purchase the paint products that you plan to use, be sure to find out what wash solvent is required, and make sure you have plenty of it on hand. You don't want to get finished spraying paint, just to find out that you don't have any reducer or thinner to clean your spray gun. Even if the place where you purchase your paint products is located next door to your shop, by the time you make the transaction, paint will be dry inside of your spray gun.

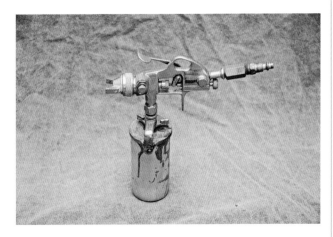

For painting hard to reach or small areas, a touchup gun works great. With a much smaller cup size than a typical spray gun, it is much easier to get into small or confined spaces. This should not be confused with an airbrush, however.

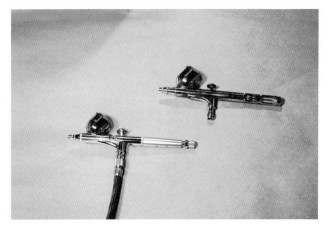

These two airbrushes are not used to paint large areas, but rather to apply very detailed artwork to any size area. The airbrush at the top is an Iwata HPC model and is used to apply relatively large areas of background or fill-in color to artwork. The airbrush at the bottom (with the air supply line attached) is a Custom Micron and is used extensively for superfine detailed artwork. Notice the extremely small paint cup size on each.

The small Makita grinder in the foreground and the larger Craftsman sander/buffer in the background make for an affordable combination for cleaning and sanding jobs. A wire cup brush attachment on the grinder will quickly remove rust, old paint, or other finishes prior to refinishing. The larger sander is commonly used with a sanding disc for prepping surfaces prior to bodywork.

To clean a spray gun, fill the gun cup partly full with solvent, then swish it around and pour out the bulk of the remaining paint products from the cup into a suitable recycling container. Refill the cup again with clean solvent and spray it through the spray gun to clean out the inner passageways. Then fill the cup about a quarter full with clean solvent and spray it through the gun until nothing but clear solvent is coming out. When that is done, clean the cup both inside and out with a cloth dampened with clean solvent. When finished, spray dry air through the spray gun to remove any lingering deposits of solvent. Now hang or set the spray gun in an upright position where it will be ready for use the next time you need it.

Tools for Sanding

You simply cannot apply paint to improperly prepared surfaces and expect it to look good. Paint itself is not designed to fill cracks, crevices, or other irregularities. Various fillers and filler-primers are available for filling the low spots, but they all require sanding prior to applying that final topcoat, in order to obtain that perfect mirror-smooth finish.

Sanding Boards and Blocks

The other reason for sanding, besides getting the surface smooth, is to eliminate surface imperfections or waves. Any area that includes custom bodywork is susceptible to waves, or high and low spots. Although waves are more easily noticeable on a larger panel, such as an automobile door, they will distract from your chopper too.

This Craftsman sander/buffer is a versatile piece of equipment that is a staple in most any shop. It can be fitted with a sanding disc to make short work of removing old paint or prepping a surface for welding. The sanding disc can be removed and replaced with a polishing bonnet for applying wax or other surface protection to painted or polished surfaces after they are finished.

A sanding block or board is an absolute necessity to keep from creating more problems than you solve. If you try to simply use your hand and a piece of sandpaper, the bones and varying amounts of pressure in your hand will actually create waves. Even though your knuckles protrude more evidently on the back side of your hand, these areas will protrude through to the inside of your hand with more pressure, while the palm will yield only a minimal amount of pressure. Sanding blocks and boards, on the other hand, provide a flexible yet rigid surface that will disperse identical pressure across the sanding material, resulting in an even surface.

Sanding boards and blocks are available in a wide variety of shapes, sizes, and materials. The smallest sanding blocks are usually made of hard rubber and are designed to use a quarter-sheet of sandpaper. These will of course be best used on smaller, confined spaces. Larger sanding boards come in different sizes and have a variety of mechanisms for securing the sandpaper. Flexible blocks often use hook and loop fasteners to secure the sandpaper, but require the use of sandpaper with comparable hook and loop backing. Other blocks are designed to be used with self-stick sandpaper, while still others use spring-loaded clips.

While most sanding blocks are flexible, some sanding boards are not flexible and therefore would see limited use on a chopper. These boards are designed more for use on automobile panels that are relatively flatter and larger than anything found on a chopper. However, if you are prepping a custom chopper that has any flat panels on it, one of these rigid "long boards" will become your best friend.

As a general rule, you should use the largest sanding block or board available for the area that you are sanding. On a surface that is wavy, a small or short block will simply ride up, over, and down each ridge. The ridges and valleys will become smoother, but they will not be getting any flatter. A longer or larger block will bridge multiple high spots and ultimately wear the high spots down, making the overall surface flatter and then smoother.

For every commercially available sanding block ever used, there is probably a one-off purely custom sanding block made by the average Joe in his home garage for a particular sanding project. For irregular surfaces, an ordinary sanding block might not get into all of the nooks and crannies that need to be sanded. Various diameters of radiator hose, paint stir sticks, or specially whittled blocks of wood have all served as impromptu sanding blocks over the years. Just don't use your hand.

For building, prepping, and ultimately painting a custom chopper, you most likely would not require the use of an air file or dual-action (DA) sander. However, should you find yourself rebuilding a wrecked bike, doing a repaint on a chopper that has already been painted, or repainting a hot rod, you may need to remove several layers of old paint, primer, and perhaps even filler material. To make quick work of this, a pneumatic sander may be desirable. Realize that this power equipment may take off body filler quicker than you desire, so use some discretion.

Sandpaper

Most everyone has some knowledge of sandpaper, but the paper used for prepping an automotive surface for paint is different from what you may have used in high school wood shop class. Most wood shop sandpaper is open coat, while most sandpaper used in automobile or motorcycle painting is for wet or dry sanding.

Open coat paper is used for rough shaping of areas where plastic body filler has been applied. Generally, 36- or 80-grit paper is used for this initial smoothing of filler.

Years ago, a cheese grater file was used, but great improvements to filler materials allow you to forego the cheese grater and start right in with the sandpaper. Progressively finer grit (numerically higher) is used until the surface is deemed smooth enough (usually 400- or 800-grit).

For general smoothing of surfaces that have not been filled, wet or dry sandpaper should be used. Like all sanding, it is used in progressively finer grits until all scratches are removed and the surface is as smooth as desired. An advantage of wet or dry paper is that it can be used with water, which helps to rinse away the sanding dust that would otherwise clog the paper.

Grits that are as coarse as 800 or lower are typically used prior to the surface being painted. Sandpaper that is finer (1,200–2,000) is typically used for color sanding the surface after the paint has been applied. This is to eliminate the surface texture of the paint itself. The key to this is to use very light pressure, a circular sanding motion, and lots of water. Using an open coat paper with water for wet sanding would simply destroy the sandpaper.

Tools for Masking

Any areas that you do not wish to paint need to be masked off. An exception is when you can actually remove the item being painted from any other surrounding components (such as removing a gas tank from the rest of the frame). The time and effort to clean off overspray will quickly overshadow any time saved by not masking. Another exception is freeform artwork, but using an airbrush should not be confused with using a spray gun . . . even if it is a detail gun.

Masking Tape

Most everyone is familiar with ordinary masking tape that is found at the local hardware store. However, that masking tape and the masking tape designed for use with automotive-type paints is drastically different. Hardware-grade masking tape works fine for taping up boxes or actually masking areas from unwanted household paint. Automotive paint grade masking tape is treated to withstand the stronger solvents used in this type of paint. These solvents can easily penetrate the weaker tape and ruin the paint finishes underneath. Additionally, adhesives used in stan-

dard-grade masking tape are not designed to easily break loose from the surface, and they can leave traces of tape and adhesive residue on the surface. Although these materials can usually be removed with mild solvents, this task may damage the paint finish underneath.

Even masking tape designed for use with automotive paints can have problems if it has been sitting on the shelf for too long. Try to buy your expendable materials from a source that does a large volume to ensure that what you use is fresh.

Masking tape ranges from 1/8 inch up to a full 2 inches in width. You most likely will not need all of the available sizes, but having two or three different widths will save you some time and aggravation. Obviously, if you need to mask something that is about 4 inches wide, it would be much easier to do with 2-inch tape than it would be with 1/4-inch tape. But, if you need to mask something that is only 1/8-inch wide, even the 1/4-inch tape will be too much.

Plastic tape is similar to masking tape, but with some specific advantages. This tape is often referred to as fine line, although Fine Line is actually the brand name of plastic tape manufactured by 3M. The difference between this tape and standard masking tape is that Fine Line is thinner and more flexible. It is not available in as many widths as masking tape. However, each width of Fine Line can go around a tighter radius curve than masking tape in a comparable width without bunching or kinking. This is what makes Fine Line tape the perfect product for laying out flames, scallops, or other artwork. While the more flexible Fine Line tape defines the outline, wider masking tape can slightly overlap the plastic tape and cover other areas.

Masking Paper

As you might imagine, masking paper is useful for masking large areas at one time. If you are going to be masking any areas that would require more than two or three strips of masking tape, you should consider using paper to mask the area. Resist the urge to simply use newspaper, as it is not appropriate for masking automotive paint materials. Newsprint is porous and therefore will allow paint to seep through, which makes it less than desirable as masking material. Some grades of newsprint also give off a type of paper-based lint that will play havoc with your painting

Any time that lots of masking is necessary, a masking paper dispenser such as this is very handy. These are available for different sizes of paper and different numbers of rolls. As the paper is pulled from the dispenser, masking tape is applied to one edge of the paper, making the paper easier to handle. You still have to tape the remaining edges, but at least the paper stays where you initially put it.

chores as well. Masking paper is treated to withstand the chemicals associated with automotive-grade paint products. Usually brown or green in color, masking paper is available in rolls from 4 inches up to 3 feet in width. Masking tape, applied by hand or directly to the masking paper when dispensed from a masking paper rack, holds the paper in place.

Transfer paper is very similar to masking paper, except that it is self-adhesive and not opaque. The fact that you can see through it makes it ideal for use when masking areas of artwork that have been outlined with plastic tape. Using an X-acto knife or razor blade, the transfer paper can easily be trimmed along the middle of the outline tape.

Other Tools

Additional items are readily available at your local paint jobber that may not be necessary, but are designed to make your tasks easier. Any time that you are mixing paint products, stir sticks and strainers are necessary. Another handy item is a mixing cup or a calibrated mixing stick. A mixing cup has calibrated markings on the outside that show the proper proportions for paint, hardener, and reducer. Several ratios are indicated, and each has indications for the necessary amounts, whether you are mixing a small or large batch. Calibrated mixing sticks are marked the same way as a mixing cup, but are held inside the cup as you add the various components. Both are used in the same way, but the mixing cup is probably easier to use while pouring in components.

Additional items that should be considered are a collection of safety related items that are discussed elsewhere in this chapter, along with hand cleaners and polishing and buffing products to be used when the painting is completed.

Materials

No one paint material is going to do everything that you need it to when it comes to painting your chopper or hot rod. Oh, yes, it would be nice if you could simply fabricate a metal creation and then just spray whatever color of paint you want on it and be done with it. That just isn't the case, so any instructions for painting must include surface preparation and the related materials as well. In addition to the multitude of brilliant colors of paint products, numerous other products must be used in specific situations to guarantee maximum color longevity, adhesion, and protection to the material that lies beneath.

If you were to simply spray paint onto the bare metal of your freshly constructed hot rod or chopper, you would not achieve the smooth finish that you might expect. It would not be long before the color would begin to wash out, perhaps peel and crack, or develop a variety of other problems.

A complete paint system from any of a number of paint manufacturers will include all of the products that are needed to complete the task. As most manufacturers have multiple lines of similar products, some of their products will cross over from one line to another. However, you

Whether you are mixing a little or a lot, a calibrated mixing cup makes mixing paint so much easier and more accurate. Paint products are designed to meet specifications, but they must be mixed as directed to achieve those goals. Simply mixing a little bit of this with about this much of that will not yield the desired results.

should not attempt to mix products from one manufacturer with those of another. By doing this, you are simply asking for trouble that just isn't necessary. From wax and grease remover, to primers, sealers, thinners, and finally base coats and clear coats, paint manufacturers design their products to be compatible with one another. Mixing sticks from each manufacturer are calibrated so that as parts of one item are mixed with others, the outcome will be a perfectly blended paint product that will serve the purposes of metal protection, paint adhesion, and color holdout as intended.

At first glance, all of the products available at an automotive paint store can be confusing. Many of the product types, such as primer or thinner, are necessary for all painting projects; others, like fish-eye preventer, are for very special circumstances. Other products, such as pearl or metal flakes, are simply designed to enhance the appearance of the material to which they are added. Before you become overwhelmed, ask the person behind the counter of your favorite auto body paint and supply store for their advice. Tell them what you are working on and what kind of finish you desire, and then ask for their advice on how to bridge that gap. They will be more than happy to tell you what products you need and how they are to be applied, and they'll send you home with some reference material.

Most paint manufacturers provide application instructions for each one of their products. These product sheets list what materials this product can be applied over as well as what can be applied over it. They also list mixing instructions and application procedures such as air pressure, drying time between coats, and cure time. These instructions also list important product safety information that is critical for safe use.

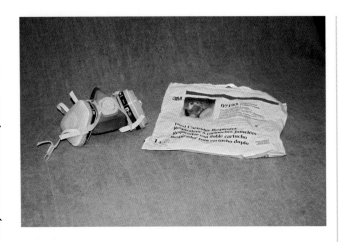

If you are going to be mixing or spraying paint, media blasting, or doing any work with any chemicals required for plating, you should be wearing a respirator with replaceable charcoal filter cartridges. The typical retail price of between $20 and $30 is simply too little to risk the dangers of not wearing one when using any of these chemicals or creating fine dust.

For Cleaning

Although painting may seem complicated to some, one thing that should be simple enough for anyone to understand is that paint products simply don't adhere well to dirt, wax, or grease. For this simple reason, any surface that is to be painted must be cleaned before each layer of primer, sealer, paint, or clear is applied.

Wax and Grease Remover

Before sanding, priming, or painting any surface, that surface needs to be as clean as possible. All traces of dirt, grease, oil, silicone, or other contaminants must be removed. If the surface is not clean prior to initial sanding, you run the risk of smearing any contaminants that are present onto a larger area and also further embedding those unwanted substances into the surface. If the surface is not clean prior to applying primer or paint, the freshly sprayed primer or paint simply will not adhere properly. Even oil from your fingers is enough to deter proper adhesion, so avoid touching the surface with your bare hands.

To obtain this clean surface, using wax and grease remover is a necessity. Wax and grease remover is readily available at your favorite paint supplier and is relatively inexpensive, so there is no reason to be without it. After using an air gun to blow away any dust or dirt that is on the surface, the wax and grease remover is applied with a clean cloth (or paper towel) or sprayed onto the surface. Wipe the surface dry, again using a clean dry cloth or paper towel. It should be apparent that the use of a clean cloth is of utmost importance here, as using any old shop towel that may have grease, brake fluid, or any other contaminants would defeat the purpose and possibly make the job worse.

Tack Cloths

Before actually spraying paint onto a surface, most professional painters use a tack cloth to remove any minute particles of dust or dirt that may have landed on the surface. If professional painters who are working in a clean, downdraft spray booth do this, you can bet that it would especially be a good idea for anyone who is painting in their home garage or other, less than Spartan, atmosphere.

Tack cloths are made of a material that is slightly tacky, hence the name. Wiping the surface with a tack cloth helps to ensure that any dust, dirt, or debris that could become trapped in the paint is removed prior to paint application. You should always open the tack cloth and hang it to allow it to air out for at least 15 minutes before using. Do not press the tack cloth hard against the surface however, as the residue may cause other problems, such as fish eyes.

Tack cloths are available at your local paint supplier. Their cost is minimal, especially when you consider the amount of dust and lint that they can remove from beneath your killer paint job.

Additives for Paint Products

Special additives for preventing potential or existing problems that you may encounter are available. Some of these additives are fish-eye preventer, chip-resistant coatings, and special additives for use on flexible components. Even though these products are available, you really don't need to concern yourself with them unless you have a specific problem. Even then, you will be better off discussing the problem with your local paint jobber and asking for their specific recommendations.

A classic example is having fish eyes (tiny rings) appear in the paint. This is typically caused by the surface being contaminated by silicone, such as from overspray from some cleaning and conditioning products. Fish-eye preventer may seem like the perfect additive to correct the situation. However, its use will actually apply more silicone to the surface and also contaminate the gun that you use to apply it. Surprising, but fish-eye preventer is like fighting fire with fire, as the preventer is actually composed of silicone. The prudent recommendation is to thoroughly wash the surface with warm water and mild dishwashing liquid before doing any prep work. After drying the surface, follow it up with wax and grease remover.

Thinners, Reducers, and Retarders

Paint pigments are solid materials held together with binders. For these substances to cure and harden into a smooth even finish, the liquid parts of the paint mixture must evaporate. To enable the solid pigments and binders to be sprayed, they are mixed with solvents, also known as thinners, reducers, and retarders.

These solvents are all designed to perform the same task. Their chemical makeup, however, is different, allowing them to work with the product for which they are designed. Thinner is designed to be used with lacquer-based products, while reducer is designed for use with enamels and urethane-based products. Since their use calls for a different chemical makeup, thinners and reducers cannot be used interchangeably.

Retarders can be either lacquer-based or enamel-based, but their chemical makeup allows for an extra-slow evaporation rate (or drying time). If you are painting in exceptionally hot weather (above 95 degrees Fahrenheit), retarder can be used to slow the drying time. This will help prevent checking, crazing, or cracking that would occur if the paint were allowed to dry too fast.

Paint products are designed to be sprayed at 70 degrees Fahrenheit and 30 percent humidity, so these would be the

Nothing says that you are required to have graphics, murals, or cartoons covering the paint on your chopper. A simple, single-color paint job complemented by some sparkle can look great.

Although it may be difficult to see in the photo, this chopper features tiny flakes of metal in the flawless red paint job. To maintain a smooth surface over these metal flakes and the black stripe, several coats of clear have been applied.

ideal conditions for your shop while painting. However, vary rarely will you have those perfect conditions for painting, unless of course you have access to a fully climate-controlled spray booth. For those of you who don't have that luxury, thinners and reducers are available in different formulas to compensate for the existing conditions in your shop. Be sure to consult your local paint jobber for the appropriate solvent for use in your particular climate.

Substrates

Substrates are the various fillers and primers that are applied to the surface material prior to actually applying paint. These layers have just as much impact on the quality of the final paint job as the paint itself.

Primer

The main purpose for primer is to promote adhesion between the surface being painted and the subsequent top coats. No one universal primer product will adequately prepare every surface for paint. Primer must be chosen for the material that it is intended to cover. Fiberglass requires different primer than aluminum, which requires different primer than galvanized steel. Some materials can be primed with regular primer, while others are better suited for epoxy primer.

Two main reasons for using epoxy primer are its superior corrosion protection and its excellent adhesion qualities. You should consult with your local paint jobber for their recommendations on the best primer for your particular needs.

Polyester Spray Body Filler

A relatively new primer product is sprayable body filler, which can be used over bare metal, aluminum, fiberglass, and most other body fillers. Since this filler-type material is thicker than most primers or paints, it will require using a spray gun nozzle tip of 2.2 (millimeters) or larger. Three or four coats should be applied, dry sanded with 120-grit, a guide coat applied (see below), and then dry sanded with 180-grit sandpaper. You should then apply another guide coat and then dry sand with 220-grit sandpaper. For the best results, you should then apply a couple of coats of primer that is suitable for wet sanding. (Ask your autobody supply and paint jobber for recommendations on a specific product.)

Primer-Surfacer

Having a high-solids content, primer-surfacers (also known as high-build primers) are used to cover slight imperfections, such as sanding scratches. These products should not be confused with or used as a filler, as they are not intended to fill more than slight scratches. Primer-surfacer is the last of the undercoat products that is designed to be sanded smooth.

After primer-surfacer is applied, it is usually block sanded smooth with 320-grit sandpaper. A second coat is then applied, allowed to dry, and then followed with a guide coat of a contrasting color of spray can enamel. This guide coat is then block sanded with 400-grit paper. This sanding will quickly remove the guide coat

To really appreciate the true color of this chopper, it would need to be seen outdoors under the sunlight. The multicolor ghost flames are readily apparent; not so obvious is the combination of pearl and metal flakes in the paint. Bear in mind that contemporary metal flakes are much smaller than those seen on fishing boats and early choppers of the 1960s.

from high spots and show low areas as well. The depth of the low spots will give a good indication whether body filler is needed or if the area can be filled with additional coats of primer-surfacer. Guide coats will be explained in greater detail in a later chapter.

Sealers

To prevent solvent from the topcoats seeping into the various undercoats, a sealer should be applied after the final undercoat has been sanded. This will add maximum adhesion capabilities and ensure uniform color match.

Sealers should also be used whenever applying new paint over a factory finish that has been baked on at high temperature. With the durability and hardness of these factory finishes, it is difficult for new paint to penetrate the surface and establish proper adhesion. If new paint is applied without first scuffing (using 180- to 220-grit sandpaper) and sealing the surface, that new paint will most likely flake off or even peel off in sheets.

Top Coats

By definition, "top coat" starts when color is actually applied, no matter how many layers of undercoats or substrates have been applied. Color may be applied with a single-stage urethane, with or without clear applied over it, or color may be applied with multistage products that are almost always top coated with clear.

Although acrylic enamel and acrylic lacquer were all the rage at one time, these products are now all but obsolete. With diligence, they can be found if absolutely necessary, such as for use on a concourse quality automobile restoration, but their use on choppers simply isn't practical. Much better products that will give much better results are now available, so there is no need to resort to old technology. However, when you are restoring a 12-cylinder 1927 Rolls-Royce Phaeton, which will be judged at events such as Pebble Beach, items such as the paint are required to be as close to original as absolutely possible. Although it may seem quite anal, judges of these events know what is available and what isn't, and judge accordingly.

Base Coats

Single-stage acrylic urethane base coats provide maximum coverage, an immediate high gloss without buffing, and a durable finish. If you plan to use a single- or dual-color paint scheme with no artwork or graphics, a urethane base coat is an ideal medium for the amateur painter. Needing only a few coats to achieve coverage, its quick-drying characteristics make simple, two-tone paint schemes easy to apply.

If show-quality shine and perfection are desired, or if graphics and artwork are going to be applied, a base coat/clear coat system would be in order. With this type of paint system, the color is applied only to achieve coverage, and it will look rather dull until the clear coat is laid down.

Clear Coats

Whether clear is applied as the second stage of a base coat/clear coat system or as an optional protective layer to a single-stage color coat, the clear is what really provides the gloss. Typically, three or four coats of clear are applied, although more coats can be applied if desired. For example, to maintain a smooth surface over metal flakes, several clear coats are needed. When clear is being applied prior to artwork, a minimum of four coats of clear should be used.

The benefit of applying clear is that unlike the color coats beneath it, the clear can be sanded with 1,500-grit or greater sandpaper to eliminate any imperfections. When sanding clear, a slight bit of dishwashing liquid should be added to a bucket of water and the surface sanded lightly using a circular motion. Taking the time and effort to wet sand the surface until it is optically "flat" (without distortion or other surface irregularities) will yield the greatest shine.

Whenever artwork or graphics are going to be applied, several layers of clear should be applied to separate the base color(s) from the artwork. With this layer of protection, an error while applying graphics can usually be repaired without getting into the paint below and causing more repair work. When extensive artwork is applied, additional coats of clear between major phases of artwork application may be justified. Think of clear coats in these instances as a "safety net" in case you make a mistake during the top coat process.

Tri-Stage Paints

Many automobiles and motorcycles are being painted at the factory with exciting colors that are now available with the use of tri-stage paints. Tri-stage paint systems are like base coat/clear coat systems, with another coat of a base color applied prior to the clear. With the number of variables, such as proper mixing, application procedure, and correct time between coats associated with the application of each coat, tri-stage paint systems are *not* recommended for the amateur painter.

Most of these tri-stage paint systems call for a base coat of silver, gold, or white to be applied. After the appropriate drying time, a second color or toner is applied. Since toners are a light mixture of color blended in with clear, the base coat will always show through this second color. This is all topped off with coats of clear, which can be sanded, buffed, and polished to achieve a lustrous shine.

With any given color of toner, it will provide a different appearance, depending on the color of the base coat beneath it. As an example, a gold base will yield a completely different final color than a silver base. Additionally, a few coats of toner over any particular base will provide a different appearance than several coats of that same toner. As you might guess, a thorough understanding of all the directions included with each stage, and some practice, is required to achieve consistent results. However, once you have perfected your ability to spray tri-stage paint, you can spray some real kick-ass colors.

Special Paints

Although the following types of paint were considered custom effects at one time, they are becoming more commonplace with the advent of tri-stage paints. However, their dazzling effects can be achieved without using the somewhat complicated tri-stage systems.

Various shades of gold and orange over a gold base provide the stunning effects on this chopper. Look at several samples when choosing colors if you plan to paint candy, as the base color will make a drastic difference in the final appearance.

Pearls

Pearl additive (actually tiny chips of inorganic crystalline substances that are painted on one side and clear on the other) can be added to clear to enhance the base color beneath. The pearl additive should be added in small amounts and test panels shot to determine the desired effect. For factory colors, your paint jobber can mix in the prescribed amount of pearl directly into the mix to replicate the color exactly. Viewing pearl paint from different angles will yield slightly different appearances, depending on the amount and color of pearl used.

Metallics (Metal Flake)

Metallic paint is achieved by adding tiny metallic flakes to the paint. Just as when mixing pearl, metallic flakes should be added a little at a time, and a test panel shot to determine the results. Spraying metallic paint requires the painter to keep the paint gun moving continuously to keep the metallic particles suspended in the paint, rather than sinking to the bottom of the spray gun. You must also use a spray gun with a larger orifice in the paint tip to avoid clogging the spray gun.

Candies

Candy colored paint is actually a tri-stage paint that is usually applied over a metallic colored base coat, such as silver or gold. To visualize the effect that a candy-type paint will yield, hold a lollypop or similar type of candy in front of a light source. You will see that the color of the lollypop will prevail, yet the color of the light source will show through.

Multicolor Paints

For truly unique color schemes, you may choose to use products such as PPG's Radiance or Harlequin, or House of Kolor's Kameleon® Kolors. These are base coats that change colors as the angle of view changes. These paints are tri-stage products that usually use a white or black base coat. Using a white base coat will provide more of a pastel appearance, while using black, dark blue, or purple as a base coat will yield more dynamic colors. Several formulas are available, with blue-to-red change and green-to-purple change being popular.

Safety Items

The paint products and tools required for most any paint job will quickly outnumber the safety-related items, but those few safety items are very important. Painting is safe, but can be harmful or even fatal if you don't respect the chemicals involved in paint products. Compared to paint products, safety items are relatively inexpensive, but would still be a bargain at twice the price, considering the potential outcome if you try to work without them.

Protecting Yourself

Everyone knows that inhaled paint fumes are not good for you, but many people don't realize that the ill effects of paint products can enter your bloodstream in other ways. Once the damage is done, it doesn't matter which safety precaution wasn't followed, so it is best to follow all of them to protect yourself.

Inhalation

All two-part paint products contain isocyanates, which are bad hombres. While many painters are still wearing only heavy-duty filter masks when spraying these components, smart painters are using full-face, fresh-air respirators for the most protection. These units may be a bit cumbersome, but for someone who paints on a regular basis, it makes good sense to learn to deal with them.

The cost of one of these fresh-air respirators might not be justifiable for someone who is painting just one project. If that is the case, you must use a proper fitting half-mask that has clean filters. Proper fit, which includes a good seal around facial hair, is the key to successful use of a half-mask. 3M manufactures disposable charcoal filter masks that are available in small, medium, and large sizes; however, they are effective for only about 72 hours after being opened.

Osmosis

One of the most overlooked ways that isocyanates can enter your body is through your eyes by way of moist tear ducts. This is another reason for wearing a full-face, fresh-air respirator, but if you don't have one, a pair of painter's goggles is a reasonable alternative.

Skin Contact

Pores in your skin are another open door in regard to isocyanates entering your body. Painter's coveralls are available in two different grades. Disposable coveralls, designed to be used only once and discarded, can be purchased for around $10. A machine washable, reusable suit can be purchased for around $65. Either way, painter's coveralls serve two functions. First and foremost, they prevent paint chemicals from contacting your skin. Secondly, the material used to make these coveralls is lint free, which means that you are less likely to have lint from your clothes affecting your paint job.

In addition to a pair of coveralls, rubber gloves and a painter's head sock will help keep isocyanates from entering your body through the pores in your skin. These safety items may not be fashionable, but neither is a casket.

Protecting the Environment

Regulations for disposal and cleanup of paint products are constantly changing, and therefore would be impossible to accurately document in this type of book. However, the auto body paint and supply store that you purchase your paint products from should have all of the current information for your particular region.

Painters in California and other regional areas are restricted to using waterborne products for most of their painting, along with a downdraft spray booth for most operations. However, if you do not live in an area that requires waterborne paint products, you most likely will not find them at your local paint supplier. The good part of this is that whatever products are available at your local paint supplier should be legally safe to use. If the product is on the shelf, you can assume it has been deemed compliant with whatever local laws are in effect.

Product Disposal

What do you do with the leftover paint products when the job is over? That will vary in your particular area; however, pouring it on the ground is a definite no-no. Some paint jobbers will dispose of your leftover paint products for a nominal fee, and you know it will be disposed of properly. Information sheets for all paint products will provide disposal recommendations, as well. If you have any questions as to the correct procedure for product disposal, you can verify what is appropriate in your area by checking with your local paint jobber or recycling center.

CHAPTER 3
PAINT: PREP TO TOP COAT

No matter how much primer and how many coats of color you may apply to a car, truck, or motorcycle, when you paint it the dents, scratches, and other surface imperfections you had hoped to cover are not going to magically disappear. In all reality, a coat of glossy paint or even dull primer will actually tend to magnify those blemishes.

Applying paint is easier for some than others, but the surface preparation is what usually makes or breaks a paint job. That preparation involves getting the soon-to-be-painted surfaces smooth and flat. (Yes, there is a difference between smooth and flat, and it will be discussed later.)

After doing whatever it takes (metal finishing or body filler) to get the surface to the shape that you want it, it must be sanded, primed, and sanded again to obtain that ever-elusive perfect finish. When that has been completed, sealer needs to be applied so that any filler that has been used does not seep through to the final paint. Then, color in the form of actual paint can be applied.

Surface Preparation

To obtain the best paint job possible, the surface has to have two distinct qualities: being clean and being straight. That first quality, being clean, is one that probably gives amateur painters their biggest headaches.

If the pieces and parts that are to be painted have an existing coat of paint on them already, they should be washed with warm soapy water to remove dust, dirt, road grime, and any other contaminants that might get in the way of allowing the paint to properly adhere to the surface. You may choose to forego the wash water to ensure you don't induce rust, if the pieces to be painted have already been stripped of paint. In either case, to make sure that the surface is clean, it needs to be wiped down with wax and grease remover prior to doing any sanding. To sand parts without first cleaning them would simply grind the contaminants deeper into the part, causing adherence problems for the paint in the future.

Before each session of sanding and before spraying any primer, surfacer, sealer, or paint, the parts that you are working on need to be dusted off with air from an air hose, and then wiped down with wax and grease remover again. Simply blowing the dust off with an air hose won't get the job done.

That second quality, getting the parts straight, is a much more involved process, but obviously every bit as important. Not only do the parts in question have to be straight (that is, free from dents and dings), but the surface also needs to be flat (smooth) for the paint to look its best.

Getting It Straight

Choppers have fewer body parts to align than hot rods or other automobiles, but what parts they do have still need to be arrow straight before paint is applied. What may look like a perfectly good fender when it is bare steel might show some minor waves or dents when a coat of primer is applied. Whether the fender is raw metal finished to perfection or steel with plastic body filler, any dents need to be removed. While a chopper is most likely going to be built from new parts, damage does occur during shipping, and sometimes it is easier to repair the part than wait for a replacement. Of course, if you had to lay a bike down for whatever reason, "building" a chopper might actually be "rebuilding," and dents are par for the course after a crash.

In addition to filling minor dents, plastic body filler is often used to fill or mold seams to make the bike's frame

PRODUCT	DESCRIPTION	CHARACTERISTICS	TYPICAL USES
Evercoat Everglass® FIB-622	Short strand, fiberglass reinforced body filler	High strength, high build, and waterproof	Repairing holes, rusted metal, body seams, and shattered fiberglass. Used as the first filler over any welds.
Evercoat Rage® Gold FIB-112	Pinhole-free body filler	Superior adhesion to galvanized steel and aluminum, high grade resin reduces risk of staining	Filling low areas of bodywork on galvanized steel or aluminum surfaces. Used as the second coat of filler over Everglass®.
Evercoat Rage® Xtreme FIB-120	Pinhole-free body filler	Self-leveling, easy spreading, easily sands with 80-grit sandpaper	Filling low areas of bodywork. Used to finish areas of Rage® Gold.
Evercoat METALWORKS® Z-Grip FIB-282	Lightweight body filler	Excellent adhesion to galvanized steel, aluminum, and epoxy primers	Filling corrosion prone areas.
Evercoat Metal Glaze® FIB-416	Polyester finishing and blending putty	Can be used over bare metal and all body fillers	Used in conjunction with other METALWORKS® body fillers and glazing putties to enhance their ease of working.
Evercoat METALWORKS® Spot-Lite® FIB-445	Lightweight finishing putty	Excellent adhesion to galvanized steel, aluminum, and plastics	Final filling of galvanized steel, aluminum, and plastics.

PAINT: PREP TO TOP COAT

appear to be one single piece of metal. Several brands and types of filler are available at your local auto body paint and supply stores. Each of these has its own particular characteristics that make each of them more or less suitable for a given situation. Some of these characteristics are speed of curing, ease of finishing, amount of pinholes that need additional filling, and adhesion qualities to particular materials, such as aluminum or fiberglass. Prior to purchasing any body filler, ask the counter person at your local auto body paint and supply store for their recommendations.

Body fillers are all applied using essentially the same methods, but you should read the directions for the particular product that you are using to be sure. Typically, the surface to be filled is sanded down to bare metal before filler is applied. Note that some fillers suggest that the surface be stripped of any paint and a coat of epoxy primer applied prior to any filler being applied. Most auto body paint and supply stores will be able to provide printed information telling you specifically which products are, and are not, compatible.

Whether you are applying filler to bare metal (or fiberglass) or to a primed surface, some amount of filler material is spread onto a mixing board or mixing sheet and then mixed *thoroughly* with a proportionate amount of hardener, using a flexible spreader. The amount of hardener to use will depend on your shop conditions regarding temperature and humidity. Experience and practice is the best way to determine how much to use, but as a start, add a 3/4-inch-wide strip of hardener across the length of the filler. Too little hardener, and it won't set up properly. Too much hardener, and it will set up right there on your mixing board. Yes, it will probably take the entire project before you learn to get the proportionate amounts just right. If you do get it mixed a little too cool (i.e., not enough hardener), you can speed the curing process slightly by placing a portable heater or heat lamp nearby. If the filler begins to "kick" before you have it spread out (too much hardener), you might as well scrape it off the mixing board and throw it away, as you won't be able to spread it properly.

45

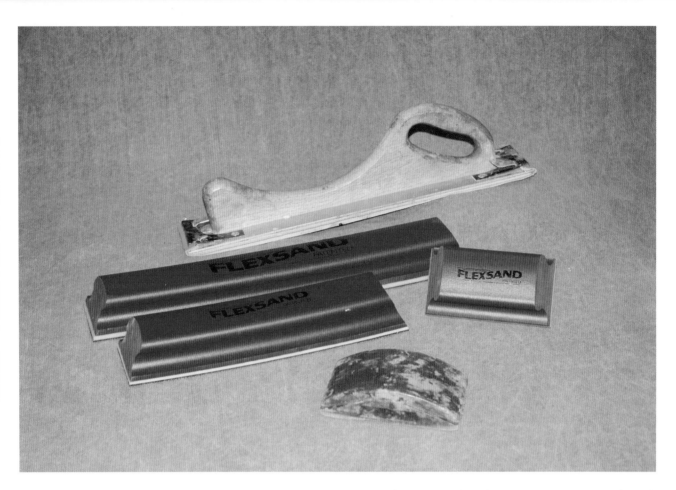

By the very nature of a chopper's construction of primarily tubular steel, the use of long sanding boards is not as common as on a hot rod. However, any time that a large surface needs to be sanded, a sanding block or sanding board should be used for best results. So, when you are sanding one of those fat rear fenders, a big ol' gas tank, or custom sheetmetal work, use some sort of sanding block (rather than just your hand) to avoid ripples in the surface.

Most body fillers use a hardener that is a distinctly different color than the filler itself, so it is easy to tell when the two are mixed thoroughly. When the mix is the same color throughout, it is well mixed. If there are streaks of color, you need to keep on mixing. When you have the filler and the hardener mixed thoroughly (all one color), scoop some filler onto a flexible spreader and spread the filler onto the area to be filled. Then make a couple of light passes over the area with an empty spreader to even out the filler.

For best results, don't apply body filler more than 1/8 inch thick total. If more than this is required, you should try to metal work the area being repaired slightly more before applying any filler. If it just isn't feasible to do any hammer and dolly work, and the area to be filled is deeper than 1/8 inch, fill it with two applications of filler, rather than attempting to fill it all at one time. Filler, like most auto

body repair products, cures as its various chemical components react and escape from the material that is left. If the filler is applied too thick, it will quite often cure on the outside before all of the chemical reaction has taken place on the inside, trapping uncured material inside of the repair. When this happens, the repair won't last the way it should and will ultimately show up in the finished paint job.

Some older types of filler require initial smoothing with a cheese grater type of file, while most newer products can be smoothed initially with 80-grit sandpaper. You should check with the person behind the counter where you purchase your products to determine the best method. If you are using any type of filler that requires using a cheese grater, you will soon realize that the initial smoothing should be done slightly before the filler cures completely. You can watch the edges of the filler to get a feel for whether it has cured enough or not. If the filler starts breaking away at the edges or if the sandpaper starts loading up, the filler has not cured sufficiently. It is difficult to describe the correct time, but with a little bit of practice, you can quickly get a feel for it. You want to knock off the high spots before the filler gets rock hard, but not too soon or you will easily gouge out more material than you really want to. As you begin working the filler, sand the entire filled area first with 80- or 100-grit sandpaper, then switch to 200- or 240-grit to blend the filler into the surrounding area. When you are finished sanding with 240-grit, you will have a good idea if more filler is necessary prior to applying primer.

When finished sanding, blow all of the sanding dust away with an air nozzle. If low spots remain, mix an ap-

propriate amount of body filler and apply it as before. Work the second and successive layers of filler (if required) just as the first until any and all low areas are filled.

Getting It Flat

Okay, you have stripped off that old chipped-up paint and filled those two big dents in the gas tank or fender. Are you ready to start spraying that new paint? As anxious as you may be to get finished, your project is probably not ready for paint yet. For paint to look its best, the underlying surface needs to be absolutely perfect.

This next step is what separates the truly professional bodywork artisans from the also-rans. This difference is going beyond getting the metal straight and going the extra

This is not meant as a self-portrait by any means, but it does show a good example of a "flat" surface in regard to painted surfaces. Obviously, the gas tank on this Harley is a collection of curved surfaces, none of which are flat in the typical sense of the word. However, look at how well the painted surface reflects the surroundings. Notice that everything is relatively distortion free, except, of course, the distortion from the curve of the tank. Getting the surface distortion free brings out the ultimate gloss of a paint job.

distance to get the surface *flat*. Almost any mirror is straight or smooth, and therefore will reflect whatever is placed in front of it with varying amounts of clarity. However, we have all seen mirrors at an amusement park that are obviously distorted to make those who look into them appear to be excessively tall and skinny, or short and fat. The reason for this distortion is that the mirrors are not flat—although they are not intended to be in those cases. If the surface to be painted is indeed flat, it will yield an almost perfect reflection. Another example of a surface that is not flat, and its effect on reflection, can be seen by taking a piece of aluminum foil and wadding it into a ball. Even though the aluminum foil can be flattened out again, it will still have a mottled surface that will greatly reduce its reflective qualities. Another example of a nonflat surface is a golf ball. Although the dimples in a golf ball are uniform, the surface is anything but flat, which would prevent anyone from obtaining a mirrorlike finish on such a surface.

So just how do you go about obtaining a flat surface prior to painting? The not-so-secret key is to use not only a sanding board or sanding block, but to use the longest one possible for the parts you are sanding. What many people don't realize, however, is that you need to sand in an "X" pattern rather than just sanding back and forth. If you simply sand back and forth, you will create a gouge. It will be smooth, but still a gouge that will ultimately need to be filled. If you are sanding in an "X" pattern that keeps moving across the panel, you will minimize your sanding time and create a flatter panel in the process.

Another reason for using a longer sanding board is that the longer board will bridge the gap between high spots, while a short sanding block will simply ride from one low spot, over the high spot, and back down into the low spots. The shorter sanding block will get the surface smooth, but not necessarily flat.

"X" PATTERN SANDING

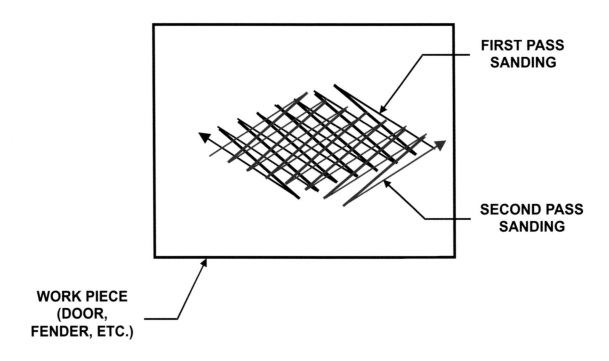

FIRST PASS SANDING

SECOND PASS SANDING

WORK PIECE (DOOR, FENDER, ETC.)

"X" PATTERN SANDING

Masking

When compared to auto body collision repair, painting a chopper or hot rod is typically easier because the latter are typically new construction, so the various pieces are already apart. Secondly, the pieces are typically smaller and easier to remove for painting, even if the painting is part of a repair. Lastly, choppers and most hot rods usually don't have the various decorative trim, body side molding, and weather stripping to contend with. Still, there is a time and place for masking, as time and effort spent to clean up errant overspray will quickly exceed that needed to mask correctly in the first place. Whenever masking is necessary, take the extra time to do it correctly and completely. A little extra time spent now will save considerable time and effort later.

Application

Other than improper surface preparation, the most common make-it-or-break-it steps in painting are in the application of the various undercoats and topcoats. This application can be further broken down into mixing, spraying, and curing. All primer/paint products have instruction sheets that provide the information needed to properly apply that particular product. You may need to ask the salesman at your local paint supply store for a copy when you purchase your painting supplies, but they will have them available. You just have to take it upon yourself to read the information that is presented to you.

Instruction sheets may or may not include sales related information such as the features, advantages, and benefits of the particular product. Data on the required products, the compatible surfaces to which it can be applied, and compatible products that can be applied to it will be included, along with safety and health information, and directions for use.

The required products are those that are required to be mixed with the particular product that the instruction sheets are describing. As an example, for PPG Concept© Acrylic Urethane, these required products include reducers and hardeners, and the instruction sheets list the appropriate options so you can choose which will be most suitable for your particular application.

Compatible surfaces are those that this particular product is designed to be sprayed upon. Since acrylic urethane is a topcoat, it is appropriate that the compatible surfaces listed are mostly primers, primer-surfacers, and sealers. For undercoats (primers), the compatible surfaces listed would include the actual material (aluminum, fiberglass, steel, galvanized steel, etc.) to which the product could be applied, in addition to other under coat products that are compatible. Instruction sheets for under coats will also include compatible top coats.

Safety and health information may be somewhat limited, but it will always include a telephone number you can call in a medical emergency or with questions about spill control. In these particular situations, someone who is knowledgeable on the product on the other end of the telephone is going to be of much more assistance than someone in your garage trying to read a bunch of fine print.

Directions for use are what allow most anyone to apply paint correctly, provided the instructions are followed accurately. Included with these directions are surface preparation, mixing ratios, additives, spray gun setup, number of coats, and drying times. Everything that you really need to know about how to apply this particular product is included on a few sheets of paper. Paper that often comes prepunched for storage in a three-ring binder, making storage for future reference very easy. Hint, hint . . .

Surface preparation tells you what to clean the surface with, which grit sandpaper to use, and everything else that should be done to the surface prior to applying the product. Mixing ratios tell precisely how many parts of reducer and/or hardener must be added to a certain number of parts of the main product. Additives describe any additional products that are designed to be used with the product and the appropriate mixing ratio. Spray gun setup provides critical information on fluid tip size, and air pressure at the cap (for HVLP guns) and at the gun (for conventional spray guns). Number of coats tells you exactly how many coats should be applied, possibly with additional notes about thickness. Drying times lets you know how long to wait between coats, how long before the surface is dust free, how long to wait before taping (for multicolor work), and how long until the product is really dry. This info is all there and can be critical to a superior paint job. You just have to take the time to read it.

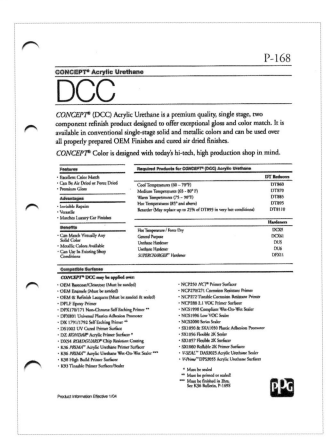

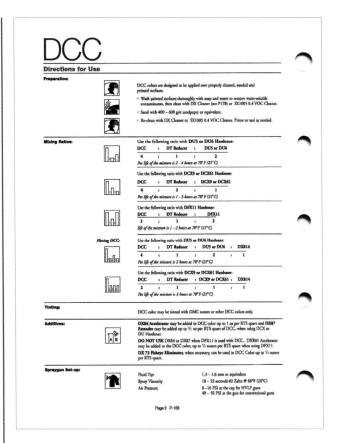

Product information sheets provide a wealth of information about the product you are about to use. Depending on the product, they may be one page or several, but certainly worth reading, no matter the length. For PPG's Concept Acrylic Urethane DCC, the first page gives a brief description of the product, as well as features, advantages, and benefits. It also lists the various components that are used as part of this particular product. At the bottom of the page, the surface treatments that are compatible are listed.

The second page provides directions for use, and is broken down into surface preparation, mixing ratios, instructions for tinting, compatible additives, and spray gun setup. This information will be necessary every time that you use this product, so a copy taped on the wall over your workbench or a copy in an easily accessible three-ring binder is a good idea.

Primer-Surfacer

After any necessary body work (such as filling seams or smoothing welds) has been completed and sanded smooth, apply glazing putty as required to fill pinholes and minute scratches. Glazing putty is very fine textured body filler that usually comes in a tube and can be spread with a plastic spreader designed for spreading body filler. After the appropriate drying time for the glazing putty (consult the directions), sand it smooth with 200-grit sandpaper. You can eliminate glazing putty by using spray poly. This provides a more uniform surface and it sands easier. However, since spray poly is a form of filler, it requires a 2.2 spray tip or larger. When the glazing putty has been sanded smooth and

there are no pinholes, spray two or three coats of primer-surfacer. Allow the proper flash time between coats and before sanding. When the surface is sufficiently dry to sand (refer to the instructions for the particular product you are using), block sand the surface with 320-grit sandpaper initially. After the entire surface has been sanded, switch to 500-grit sandpaper and block sand the entire surface again. Now check for sand scratches or shallow low spots (significant low spots require more filler, but should be gone by this time). To these areas, apply two or three additional light coats of primer-surfacer. Sand again with 320- and 500-grit sandpaper.

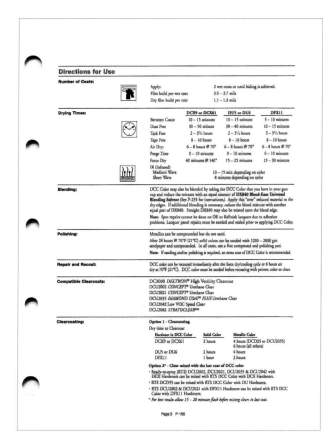

More directions are found on the third page. These include the recommended number of coats, drying times, instructions for blending and polishing, as well as information on clear coating.

The last page includes technical data and company addresses that you may not care about. However, it also lists very important information . . . such as a telephone number to call in a medical emergency or for spill control information. With proper instructions and an eye on safety, you may never need this last information, but it is nice to have should the unexpected happen.

Now apply a guide coat by dusting on a contrasting color of spray-can enamel. You do not need to achieve full coverage with this guide coat. It should be applied evenly, but merely fogged on. When this guide coat has dried, sand it off using 600-grit sandpaper. Sanding will quickly remove the guide coat from high spots and will quickly show low areas as well. The depth of the low spots will give a good indication whether body filler is needed or if the area can be filled with additional coats of primer-surfacer. High spots can be removed by additional sanding.

Sealer

For all intents and purposes, applying sealer is the last step before applying color topcoats. No more sanding is necessary (or advised) until clear is applied, or unless you are required to sand out a run or other screw-up. This means that any custom bodywork must be arrow straight prior to receiving sealer. Any sanding scratches, runs in the primer, or any other surface imperfections that can be seen now are there to stay, once the sealer is applied, so they need to be addressed . . . now. Go ahead, I'll wait. Okay, now that everything is as smooth as your significant other's bottom, sealer should be applied.

This rolling chassis chopper is for sale, so there is no need for the owner/builder to go to the expense of painting it. However, to provide surface protection in the meantime and perhaps to give a more finished look, the steel frame, tank, and fender have been coated with epoxy primer.

The sealer serves two major purposes. For one, the sealer keeps any solvents from the impending topcoats from seeping into and damaging the undercoats beneath. Secondly, sealer improves adhesion and color uniformity for the topcoats. Apply the sealer per the manufacturer's recommendations, allow it to cure properly, and then get ready to spray color.

Base Color Coats

Okay, you have fabricated the wheeled wonder of your dreams, and perhaps even taken it out for a ride in its raw, unpainted form. Now you have disassembled everything, ground all the welds down to perfection, and block sanded every piece that is to be painted. The time has come . . . it's time to get this thing painted!!! This certainly is a milestone to be proud of reaching. If you have gotten this far, you can make it the rest of the way fairly easily, but you sure don't want to botch it up now. Preparation is and always will be the key to the perfect paint job, but that doesn't mean that you can finish the job haphazardly and expect great results.

By now you should be familiar with your spray gun and how it should be adjusted for spraying the various primers and undercoats that you have applied thus far. If you have not yet sprayed any color, or if it has been a while and you feel out of practice, find something other than your pristine project parts to practice on. Paint is different than primer . . . it covers differently and it runs quicker. It is much better to leave the amateurish runs, drips, and other paint irregularities on a practice panel (or several) and paint your chopper or hot rod like a pro. Make sure that your spray gun is thoroughly cleaned and adjusted properly.

Before mixing the paint and filling your spray gun, take a few extra minutes to review the instruction sheets for the paint you are using. Highlight the time-frame recommendations and other important information so that you can refer to it easily when needed. Between coats is not the time to frantically look all over your garage for this information.

Paint Mixing

To take the guesswork out of paint and solvent mixing, paint manufacturers have designed calibrated mixing sticks. According to mixing directions, an amount of paint is poured into a clean, empty can with straight sides (not a spray gun cup) up to a certain number located along one vertical column on that paint system's designated mixing stick. Solvent is then poured in until the fluid level in the can rises to a corresponding number on the next column over on the same stick. Clear mixing cups with calibrations printed on them are used in the same manner as mixing sticks.

If a one-to-one ratio of paint to solvent mixture were indicated on label directions, for example, paint would be poured into an empty can up to the number one. Reducer is added until that total mixture reaches the number one on the next column over. If more paint is needed, because of a large job, simply mix the ingredients up to a higher number.

When using a paint system that requires mixing paint, solvent, and hardener, a corresponding mixing stick is required. Instead of just two columns of numbers, it will have three. Again, paint is poured to the appropriate number, depending on the amount of material needed for the job. Solvent is poured in until the fluid level rises to the identical number in its column, and then hardener is added until the content reaches the same number in the hardener column. As far as hardener is concerned, once it mixes with paint, the hardening process begins. As you will note on application guides and information sheets, catalyzed paint has a pot life of only so long. Hardener, therefore, is mixed with paint only just before spraying begins.

Not all paint systems are based on a one-to-one ratio. By looking at a paint-mixing stick, you will see that sometimes the numbers on the reducer or hardener are not twice as high up the stick as those in the paint column. Mixing paint, solvent, and hardener is an exact science. You must follow the manufacturer's recommendations and instructions to be assured of a quality blend.

Once your paint product has been carefully blended, use the stir stick to swish the contents around in the mixing can. Pointed tools, like screwdrivers, are not recommended for stirring. The flat-bottomed, rather wide nature of stir sticks works best. Stir for at least two minutes. Then place a paint filter over the opening of your spray gun cup and pour in the mixture. It is important that you never, repeat, *never*, pour paint into your spray gun cup without using some type of filter. If you were to do so, dust, dirt, or dried paint from the top of the can could fall into your spray gun cup, causing a clog that would be difficult to remove. Your paint product is now ready for spraying. Be sure to put the caps back on containers of solvent and hardener, as well as the paint. This will preserve your paint for next time by preventing unnecessary evaporation or accidental spillage.

In the paint booth, tack off the surface to be painted immediately, then start painting. Some paint products and colors are designed with a lot of heavy solids that could settle to the bottom of paint cups in just 10 to 15 minutes. If you were to take your time tacking and then wait a little longer while your paint gun sat idle, solids could settle, possibly causing the color to change. This would be a catastrophe.

Spray Gun Controls and Test Patterns

The high-tech world of automotive painting extends past basic paint material mixtures and safety equipment to the fluid tip and air cap dimensions of spray paint guns. Companies such as PPG recommend specific spray gun setups for application of their products. Such a specification is this recommendation for base coat spray guns: "DeVilbiss JGV-572; Fluid Tip – FW (0.062 in.); Air Cap #86." The same kind of recommendations follow for primer and clear coat spray guns involving DeVilbiss, Sata, and Sharpe gun models. You can obtain this information from information sheets and application guidelines. Or, check with your paint supply jobber.

Two control knobs are typical on most full-size production spray paint guns. One controls the fan spray, while the other manages the volume of paint that exits the nozzle. They are located at the top rear section of most models. About the only way to determine proper spray patterns and volume combinations is to practice spraying paint on a test panel. Various paint products and their reduction ratios will spray differently, especially when recommended air pressures vary.

To assist in perfecting fan and volume match, many painters keep test panels in their spray paint booth. Usually,

No doubt about it, painting wheels can be a challenge. Many painters will hang wheels whenever they are applying primer, sealer, or paint, but quite often, this results in a small spot being missed where the wire used to hang the wheels makes contact with the wheel. One way to avoid this is by setting the wheel in the horizontal position on top of a paint can. This method takes longer, because you can only paint one side at a time and must allow each coat to dry completely before flipping the wheels over.

these are nothing more than sheets of wide masking paper spread and taped to a wall. On the test panel, they can spray paint and then make adjustments to control knobs until just the right pattern and volume are established. At that point, they begin actual painting.

Periodically during paint jobs, painters may notice a flaw in their gun's fan pattern. To check it, they turn to the test panel and shoot a clean section with a mist of paint. If the pattern is not uniform, it is noticed immediately. Controls are checked, as well as the air pressure. If the pattern is still flawed, the paint gun is disconnected from the supply hose and cleaned. Chances are, a small port or passage has become clogged and must be cleaned before the job can continue.

Spray Gun Maneuvering

Spray paint guns apply their most uniform and effective paint finishes when they are held perpendicular to the surfaces being sprayed at a distance of 6 to 10 inches. However, you should check the recommendations for your particular spray gun. PPG's *Refinish Manual* clearly states, "If the gun is tilted toward the surface, the fan pattern won't be uniform. If the gun is swung in an arc, varying the distance from the nozzle to the work, the paint will go on wetter where the nozzle is closer to the surface and drier where it is farther away." This all adds up to imperfect or blemished paint finishes because some of the product dries just microseconds before it reaches the surface, while other parts of the same fan spray go on wetter than intended.

SPRAY OVERLAP

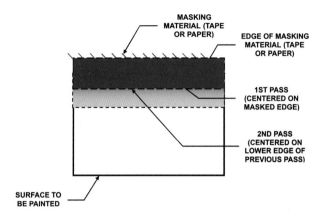

MASKING MATERIAL (TAPE OR PAPER)

EDGE OF MASKING MATERIAL (TAPE OR PAPER)

1ST PASS (CENTERED ON MASKED EDGE)

2ND PASS (CENTERED ON LOWER EDGE OF PREVIOUS PASS)

SURFACE TO BE PAINTED

SPRAY OVERLAP

Even fan spray should overlap the previous spray by half. In other words, the center of the first pass should be directed along the masking line: half of the paint on the masking paper, the other half on the body surface. The second pass should be directed in such a way that the top of the fan rides right along the masking line. Then, each successive pass should overlap the previous one by half. Maneuver each pass with the same speed and at the same distance away from the surface: 6 to 10 inches.

Look at your painting results. If you have practiced with your equipment on an old practice panel, chances are good that your efforts are proving worthwhile. If not, you might be experiencing runs or other gross abnormalities. Runs are generally caused by too much paint landing on the surface at one time. You may be holding the gun too close or moving it too slowly. Whichever, you have to adjust your technique. This is where practice will get you in shape for perfecting paint-spraying maneuvers.

Flash Time

Paint dries by allowing its solvent to evaporate and its pigments to cure. For this reason, you must not apply additional coats until the previous coats have had sufficient time to evaporate. If additional coats are applied too soon, this will trap solvents beneath the second coat. However, these solvents will not merely stay in place, rather they will continue to work their way out to the atmosphere, causing blistering, cracking, dulling, or other imperfections to appear in the top coat.

The necessary flash times (the time between successive coat applications) are clearly indicated on the application instructions for all paint products. Second and final coats may require longer flash times than initial coats, but you should check the application instructions to be sure.

Clear Coat Finishes

Applications of clear over a colored base allow for much more gloss than single-stage paints. The main reason for this is that after applying four coats of clear, each coat of clear thereafter can be wet sanded to a mirror-smooth surface. Additionally, the clear provides more protection for the paint (including artwork) beneath it. Any scratches to the clear coat that do not penetrate completely through to the paint below can be repaired without the need to apply additional paint.

Clear is applied in the same manner as any other paint. It is mixed with a hardener in a specific ratio, sprayed at a recommended air pressure, and allowed to flash dry a recommended length of time between coats, all of which is specified on the application instructions. The biggest challenge to spraying clear is maintaining uniformity in each coat. Since the clear has no pigment, it is often difficult to determine how much or how little you are actually applying. You don't want to have runs in the clear, but you do want ample coverage. Good lighting and ample practice will help to overcome these obstacles—use the same spray gun maneuvering technique you just used to lay down that brilliant base color coat.

Drying Times

No two ways about it, automotive and motorcycle paint has to dry. If not allowed to do so in a clean environment, dust, dirt, or other debris could still penetrate wet surfaces, ruining all of your hard work in the process. Professional painters always leave freshly sprayed vehicles in paint booths until enough time has elapsed for the material to completely cure. Specific time frames are included on product labels and application guides.

For example, PPG recommends their DCC Acrylic Urethane paint systems be allowed to dry 6–8 hours at 70 degrees Fahrenheit, or be force dried for 40 minutes at 140 degrees Fahrenheit. Force drying requires the use of portable infrared heaters or high-tech paint booths equipped with heating units. For their Deltron base coat and clear coat systems, PPG lists specific drying times for air drying, as well as force drying, for each of the products used in the system. This is critically important information, especially when base coat materials have already been sprayed, and you need to determine exactly when the clear coat can effectively be applied. Other factors must also be considered when using heat lamps and other force dry methods. Of great importance are initial flash times. Most paint products must air dry for 15 minutes, or longer, to let the bulk of solvent material evaporate on its own. In these cases, too much heat applied too soon will cause excessive solvent material to evaporate much too fast, resulting in blemishes to the paint finish.

All of the information you need to make determinations on how long to wait (drying time) before wet sanding or buffing is supplied through information sheets and application guides provided by paint manufacturers. Along with recommendations on how long to wait before wet sanding or recoating, there are specific time frames related to how much time is allowed to elapse before these chores will not be effective. You have a window of time to work with. Waiting too long, in other words, may require some finishes be scuff sanded and cleaned before application of touchup paint coats.

Color (Wet) Sanding

Not every type of paint system can accept wet sanding. Enamels, for example, cure with a sort of film on their surface, which will be damaged if broken by sandpaper or harsh polish. You have to wait about 90 days before polishing enamels.

Base coat/clear coat paint systems generally call for a number of color coats and then clear coats. Especially with candy finishes, sanding directly on the color surface will distort the tint to cause a visible blemish. Wet sanding for them is done on clear coats only. Your wet sanding efforts should be concentrated on clear coats in order to not disturb the underlying color coats. Wet sanding clear coats will bring out a much deeper shine and gloss when followed by controlled buffing and polishing.

Start with very fine 800-grit and work up through 3,000-grit sandpaper with water, using a circular motion to smooth or remove minor blemishes on cured paint finishes designed to allow wet sanding. Only sandpaper designated wet-or-dry must be used, however. Those kinds that are not waterproof will fall apart and be useless.

As with all other sanding tasks, you have to use a sanding block, although it should be smaller than the typical sanding block used for smoothing bodywork. Folding sandpaper around a wooden paint stir stick instead of using a large hand block is common practice. Only a small amount of pressure is required for this type of delicate sanding.

Be sure to dip sandpaper in a bucket of water frequently to keep the paint surface wet and reduce the amount of material buildup on the sandpaper. Add a small amount of mild car washing soap to the water bucket to provide lubrication to the sandpaper. The sandpaper should be allowed to soak in water for 15 minutes before wet sanding. You should also be sure to use clean water. Some water supplies, whether city or rural, have small mineral deposits that you don't want being pushed around on your new paint job. To combat this, let the bucket of water sit overnight so that the contaminants can settle to the bottom before using it.

If a lot of sanding was needed on certain blemished areas, new coats of clear may have to be applied. This is why you should leave masking material in place while accomplishing wet sanding chores. Should clear coat touchup be needed, the vehicle will already be masked, saving extra masking work.

You must confirm ahead of time that the paint system you use is compatible with light wet-sanding repair efforts. Your paint supplier can do this while you are discussing your paint needs at the time of purchase. Each paint manufacturer has its own set of recommended guidelines it advises painters to follow. What may be good for PPG's Deltron system may not be so good for a BASF or DuPont system. In fact, you might even be advised to completely disregard wet sanding and opt instead for polishing to guarantee a perfect finish with the type of product that you have chosen to use.

Removing Masking Material

Masking materials must be removed in a controlled manner to prevent unnecessary finish damage. By now, you should fully understand that paint products have solids in them that build up on car bodies. Especially on jobs where numerous color and clear coats were applied, the thickness of the paint can bridge the lips along masking tape edges. What will occur, in some situations, is the formation of a paint film that continues over to include the top of the tape. Therefore, if tape is pulled straight up, it could take with it flakes of paint from the body surface.

To prevent paint flaking or peeling along the edge of masking tape strips, pull tape in a direction away from the newly painted surface and back upon itself to create a sharp angle at the point where tape leaves the surface. In a sense, the sharp edge of the tape and this sharp angle can "cut" extra-thin paint films, instead of pulling them away and causing flakes or cracks on the finish.

Rub Out and Buffing

As with wet sanding, not every type of paint system can stand up to vigorous polishing or rubbing out. You must confirm the compatibility (and need) for extensive polishing with your paint supplier before starting the procedure. In cases of single-stage urethane, buffing new paint with a gritty compound will only dull the surface and ruin the finish. In contrast, polishing a catalyzed urethane (base coat/clear coat) or cured lacquer might make their finishes much more brilliant, lustrous, and deep shining as the polishing process smoothes away the tiniest of imperfections in the paint itself.

A wide variety of polishing compounds are available for use on new paint finishes. Autobody paint and supply stores carry the largest selection. Some are designed to be used by hand, while others can safely be polished with buffing machines. Foam pads work best with prescribed compounds and buffing machines limited to slower rpm, while pads made with cloth material are better suited for other compounds and machine speeds. For a complete breakdown of all the different compounds, pads, and buffing machines, visit an auto body paint and supply store.

Although other brands are available, a suggestion would be to begin with a wool pad, Mirror Glaze 85 compound, and a buffer speed of 1,200 to 1,400 rpm. Then use a Mirror Glaze 8000 foam pad with dual-action compound at 1,600 to 1,800 rpm, followed up with a Mirror Glaze 9000 foam pad to apply 3M Perfect It II or III. Finish up by hand with Mirror Glaze Hand Polish.

PPG manufactures their own brand of rubbing and polishing compounds designed to be compatible with their paint system products. You should never go wrong using them with PPG paints. In addition, companies like 3M and Meguiar's produce several varieties of polishing products, all of which carry labels with specific instructions for their intended use and application.

Basically, rubbing compounds include relatively coarse polishing grit material. They are designed to quickly remove blemishes and flatten paint finishes. Because of the compounds' coarse nature, light scratches, also called swirls, will be left behind on paint finishes. Therefore, after an application of compound to flatten orange peel or produce a higher surface luster, paint finishes need to be buffed or polished with a very fine grit material. In some situations, especially with dark colors, this is accomplished with exceptionally soft finish buffing pads and wax.

As refinish products have changed over the years, some ideas that seem like common sense are no longer valid. With the new urethane paint products, it is suggested that you polish with 2,000-grit compound using a foam pad. This should minimize swirls and yield a satisfactory finish the first time around. If swirls are still present, you should go back to a slightly coarser compound to remove the swirls, then use the finer 2,000-grit again. Older technology would have said to use the coarse rubbing compound first, then work up to the finer stuff, instead of this seemingly backward procedure. If you begin getting swirl marks, go back to a finer compound.

Although paint finishes may appear dry, especially those that included a hardening agent, they may not be ready for buffing right away. You must allow sufficient time for all solvents to evaporate before smothering them with polishing compound. Application guides and information sheets will generally list the recommended time. The information sheet for PPG's polyurethane clear, for example, states, "Allow 16 hours before polishing either air dried or force dried DCU 2021."

By hand, use a soft, clean cloth for rubbing out and polishing, and follow directions on the product label. You need experience and practice with a buffing machine before using it on your new paint job. Buffers with maximum speeds of about 1,450 rpm are best for novices. Machines with faster revolutions require more user experience to prevent the likelihood of paint burns—accidentally polishing through paint finishes down to primer or bare metal. Be aware, though, even the slower 1,450-rpm buffers are quite capable of causing paint burns if users do not pay attention to what they are doing.

To use a buffer, first spread out a few strips of compound, each about 4 to 6 inches apart to cover an area no bigger than 2 square feet. Operate the buffing pad on top of a compound strip and work it over that strip's area, gradually moving down to pick up successive strips. The idea is to buff a 2-square-foot area while not allowing the pad to become dry of compound. Buffing continues on that section until the compound is gone and all that remains is shiny paint.

Buffing pads can be operated back and forth, as well as up and down. Always keep them moving. Just like power sanders, if buffers are allowed even momentarily to rest in one spot, the chances for paint burns greatly increase. Likewise, be exceptionally careful buffing near ridges, gaps, and corners. The swift rotation of buffing pads will quickly burn paint on these areas. Don't operate a buffing pad on top of ridges; run it just up to the edge and stop. Some painters prefer to mask edges, ridges, and corners with strips of masking tape to protect them against accidental buffing burns. This is a good idea for the novice.

Power buffers will throw spots of compound all over your car, clothes, and nearby surfaces. Be prepared for this kind of mess by covering adjacent cabinets or workbench items with tarps or drop cloths. Always wipe buffing

Some graphics are subtle, while others are not. Multiple layers of graphics add lots of visual impact to this chopper. Notice how the black frame virtually disappears in relation to the larger sheetmetal areas of this bike.

compound thrown by the buffer off the paint as soon as possible, as it can damage the new paint if it is allowed to dry.

As cloth buffing pads become covered with compound, or every three passes (whichever comes first), you should use a pad spur or buff rake to clean them. With the pad spinning, gently but securely push a spur into the pad's nap. This will break loose compound and force it out of the pad. You will be surprised at how much material comes off of pads, so be sure to do your pad cleaning away from anything that you don't want covered with compound or pad lint. You cannot clean the buffing pads too much.

Overspray

Polishing and buffing efforts usually work well to remove very light traces of overspray. Extra-heavy overspray residue may require a strong polishing compound for complete removal. For severe problems, consult your paint supplier.

Graphics

A well-designed hot rod or chopper coated with flawless paint and highlighted with a tasteful amount of plated and polished components will look great all by itself. But, when you start hangin' out with your buddies, all those equally nice rides will start looking alike. Next thing you know, somebody adds some flames. This looks nice, but then somebody decides to do them one better and adds some airbrush work. Next thing you know, nobody's hangin' out anymore—they're all back at their shops laying down some flames or airbrushing pinup girls on their rides. Graphics have gotten to the point where there is absolutely no limit to the creativity, complexity, or colors you can use.

Except for purely custom one-off creations, choppers and hot rods are often a collection of mass-produced pieces. The slight differences are the combinations of parts used and the final colors and processes used to finish them. Graphics and artwork are the truly unique features that add the individual personality of those who build and ride them.

LAYING OUT FLAMES, MASKING, AND PAINTING

For a slick method of applying flames, follow along as Tim Kohl at Mayhem Custom Paint & Graphics adds hot licks to a chopper gas tank. Tim obviously has artistic talent and experience, but the method that he uses could be duplicated by almost anyone and on almost anything with a little bit of practice. This method isn't the only way to obtain these results, but it works well for Tim.

The basic plan is to paint the tank (in this case) with a base coat of purple, and then clear coat it. Whenever applying any sort of artwork, a clear coat between the base color and the artwork is cheap insurance and goes a long way toward minimizing the effort required to repair any mistakes.

After the appropriate curing time, the entire surface of clear coat is scuffed with 800-grit sandpaper.

The flames are laid out using 1/8-inch Fine Line tape. The entire tank is masked, and then the masking removed from the flame areas. The color of the pinstripe separating the flames from the base color is applied with an airbrush. That pinstripe is then masked and the color for the flames applied. After the appropriate drying time, the masking materials are removed and clear applied to bring out the original color of the tank, along with the gloss. Now follow along as we go over it one step at a time.

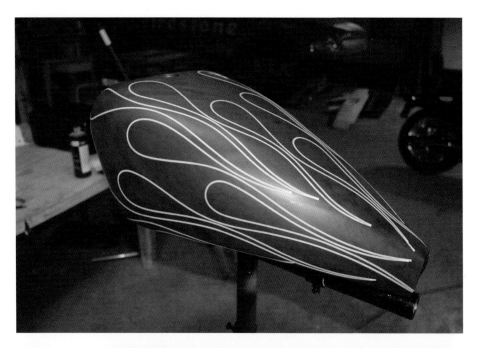

Tim Kohl had already laid out the flames on one side of this tank when I arrived, but we'll follow Tim as he lays out the remaining licks. Prior to applying the Fine Line tape, the tank has been painted with a base coat of purple along with a clear coat, and then the clear coat scuffed with 800-grit sandpaper so that the new paint (for the flames) will adhere properly.

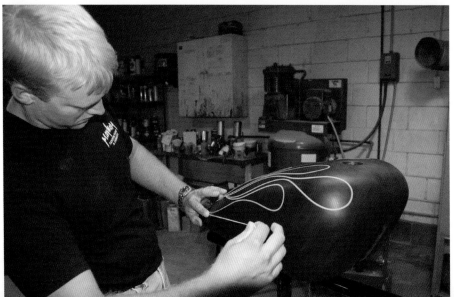

Tim uses 1/8-inch-wide Fine Line tape to lay out the flames. Real flames are not symmetrical, so painted flames don't have to be either, although they should be balanced side to side. If it is desired for the flames to be the same on both sides, it could be done by creating a pattern of one side and then transferring it to the other side with pounce and a pounce wheel.

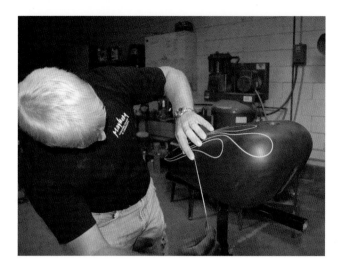 

On larger panels, such as a car hood and fenders, it may be desirable to use some Fine Line tape to make some reference lines to assist in keeping the layout of the flames uniform. However, on a small item such as a motorcycle tank, Tim lays the flames out completely freehand, albeit with an experienced eye.

Tim pulls the Fine Line tape out ahead of where it will be on the tank, and then presses it into place with his free hand. Fine Line tape can be easily pulled back up and repositioned if the layout isn't quite what you want.

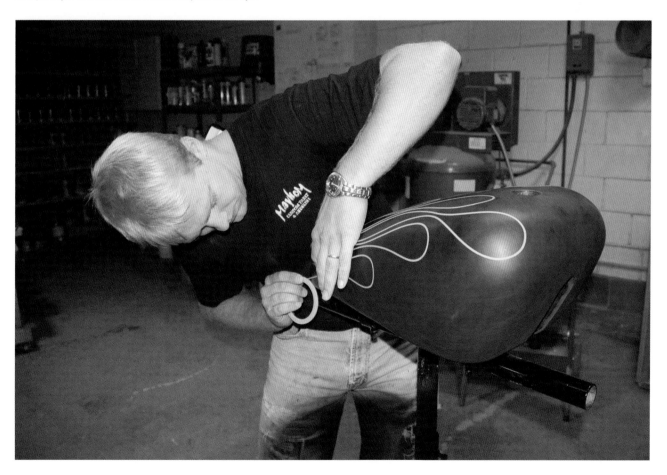

To achieve balance from one side to the other, Tim often refers to the first side. Each piece of tape runs from one flame tip, around the belly, and ending at the next flame tip, so that the ends of the tape are naturally running in a straighter direction than if the tape ended in the belly of the flame.

Notice that Tim uses a tank stand that can be rotated from side to side. This provides for easier access to the lower surfaces of the tank, allowing more efficient preparation and finishing.

After the entire flame layout has been outlined with 1/8-inch Fine Line tape, the entire surface of the tank is covered with self-adhesive transfer paper.

Transfer paper is similar to frisket paper, which is self-adhesive paper used for masking. The main difference between the two is that frisket paper is opaque. Transfer paper is not clear, but the Fine Line tape already on the tank can be seen through it.

The size of the tank dictates the use of a second piece of transfer paper. It is applied in the same manner as the first, making sure that there is plenty of overlap of the first and second pieces of paper. Tim takes his time to make sure that the transfer paper makes good contact with the surface to be masked, but especially near the flame edge where the edges will eventually be exposed.

Unlike the upper portion of the gas tank, the lower portion makes a relatively sharp turn at the bottom. With the taper of the tank and the sharp turn, this would be difficult to mask with paper, so the excess transfer paper is cut off with a razor blade.

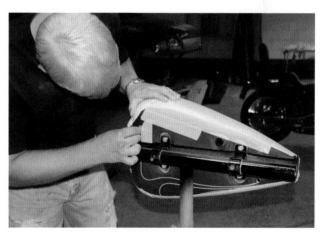

Tim covers the remaining underside of the tank with strips of standard 1-inch-wide painter's masking tape. Note that the flames carry over completely to the bottom of the tank, as seen by the outline on the right side of the tank.

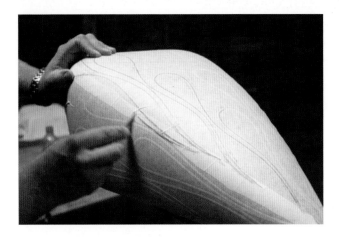

The 1/8-inch Fine Line tape can be seen through the transfer paper, but to make the tape easier to follow with a razor blade, Tim rubs the side of a pencil over the tape, making the flame layout much easier to see.

Even from a distance, the flame layout can be seen while Tim cuts the transfer paper along the Fine Line tape that delineates the flames. The object is to cut in the middle of the tape, but not through the tape. As long as the cut is somewhere between the two edges of the tape (and not through) the smooth edge of the Fine Line will still be the edge of the painted flames.

With the transfer paper cut along the edges of the flames, Tim begins removing the transfer paper from the tank.

With all of the necessary transfer paper removed, you get a preview of the flames. The unmasked areas will be painted silver metallic, while the masked areas will remain purple. The greenish yellow near the back of the tank is masking tape used to ensure that any errant cuts made near the ends of the flame tips are covered and don't allow for any silver slivers near the flame tips.

To remove any transfer paper adhesive, skin oil, or anything else that may prove to be a detriment to paint adhesion, Tim wipes down the tank with wax and grease remover.

After wiping the wax and grease remover off with a clean cloth or paper towel, an air hose is used to ensure that all of the wax and grease remover is wiped away or air dried.

Next, Tim uses a tack cloth to pick up any dust particles that may have landed on the surface to be painted.

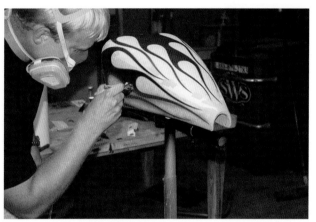

The tank will be deep purple with silver flames, and a lavender pinstripe separating the two. The pinstripe could be applied by brush after the flames are painted, but Tim prefers to apply the pinstripe with an airbrush prior to painting the flames.

Tim will be using a 1/16-inch pinstripe, so the lavender color is applied to the outer edges of the flames approximately 1/8 inch wide.

Three coats of the lavender color for the pinstripe are applied, allowing the appropriate drying time between coats.

To achieve a uniform 1/16-inch pinstripe, 1/16-inch Fine Line tape is applied just inside of the tape that delineates the flame itself. After the flames are painted and the Fine Line tape removed, the lavender pinstripe will remain.

Extreme care must be taken to ensure that the 1/16-inch Fine Line (pinstripe) perfectly abuts the 1/8-inch Fine Line (layout). If there are any gaps between the two tapes, the area in between will be painted silver.

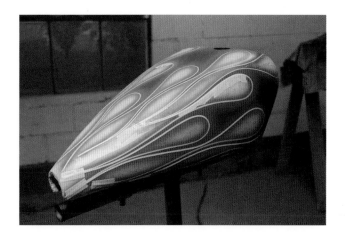

Unless, of course, you cover minor gaps with strips of masking tape. Make sure that the tape is mashed down flat against the surface . . . especially in sharply curved areas, where the tape will tend to buckle.

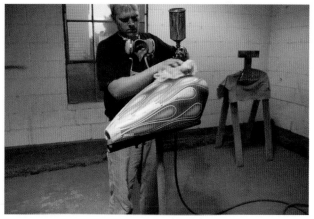

Prior to painting the flames, Tim cleans the area again. First with wax and grease remover and then with a tack cloth.

PAINT: PREP TO TOP COAT

67

With the exhaust fan running and respirator mask on, Tim applies the first of three coats of silver metallic base coat to the flame area. Be sure to apply multiple light coats, rather than one heavy coat.

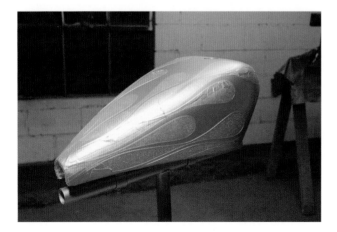

Apply enough base coat to achieve full coverage. The high gloss you are aiming for will be a result of the clear that will be applied later.

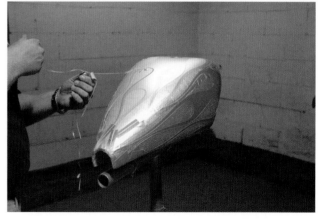

Refer to the instruction sheets provided with the specific paint products you are using to determine the correct time between coats, appropriate tape time (that is the time the paint must dry before removing masking tape), and final cure time. When you do remove tape, try to pull the tape and other masking materials away from the surface at a 90-degree angle whenever possible.

After allowing sufficient time for the base coat to dry, Tim begins to remove the masking materials. He will remove enough of the masking material from the top of the tank so that I can show you the flame layout, but will let the paint fully cure before handling the tank to remove the tape from the lower side.

Tim says that unmasking a flame job is like opening a Christmas present . . . you can't wait to see what is underneath all the paper.

Other than being on the completely assembled chopper, the only difference in the tank from the preceding photo is that several layers of clear coat have been meticulously sanded.

FREEHAND AIRBRUSH

In addition to flames that are masked and very precise, Tim Kohl at Mayhem Custom Paint & Graphics is also very talented with an airbrush. For this particular fender, the owner wants to have a faded version of Old Glory blowing in the wind. He doesn't want it to look like Captain America or anything that might become overbearing, but yet something more than just a ghost image. This is a very time-consuming process with perhaps little differences noticeable from one photo to the next, but from beginning to end, the differences are quite stunning.

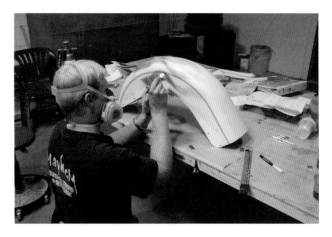

Tim Kohl has already applied a light blue field for the stars of Old Glory and has begun adding the red and white stripes. Making this task a bit more difficult is the fact that the flag needs to be waving in the breeze. The stripes are roughed in lightly in the beginning.

The stripes have been heavied up and are taking on a three-dimensional look. With the basic flag colors of red, white, and blue roughed in, you can see that it is a flag, but still requires more work before it is finished.

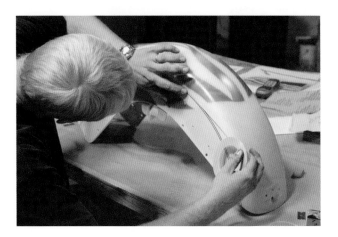

An existing stripe on the side of the fender is to remain, so it is masked off from receiving additional paint by adding a strip of Fine Line tape.

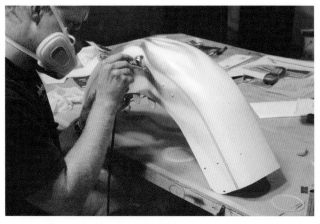

As a real flag would be waving, portions of the stripes would appear darker, while other portions would appear lighter. Tim re-creates this appearance by adding more red to the brighter areas.

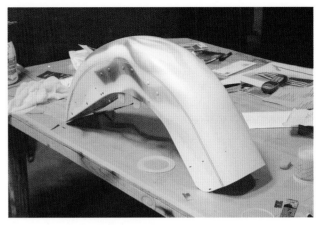

The appearance of the flag also depends on the positioning of the fender. The red stripes are somewhat brighter on the top of the fender than down on the sides. A subtle difference, but an important one.

Notice how the red stripes (painted) and the white stripes (not painted) have a two-dimensional look at this point. The stripes simply appear to be bands of color that vary in width.

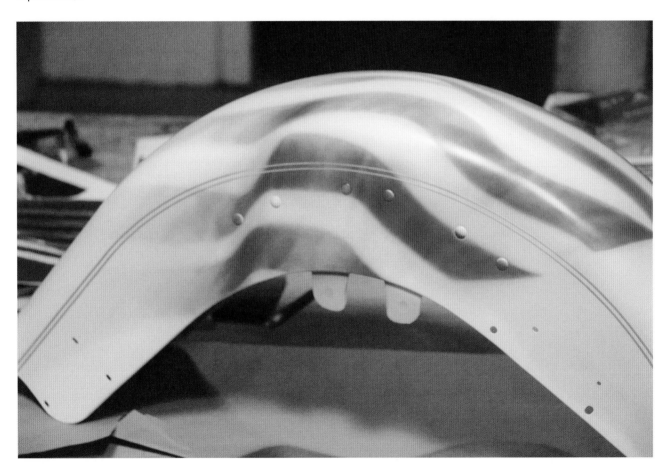

By adding light gray streaks to both the red and the white stripes, the material of the flag itself magically appears. This also increases the three-dimensional effect, as it provides more of an indication as to which direction the material of the flag is running.

In this second set of photos, Tim Kohl is in the process of adding graphics to various components of a chopper that has already been built. This method requires disassembly and could have been done when the chopper was built originally . . . but that is between the owner and the painter. The skulls and reptile are purely from the mind of Mayhem, who has applied all of the artwork from scratch.

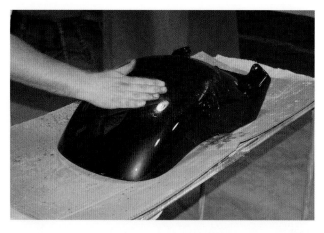

Using 800-grit wet or dry sandpaper, the clear coat is scuffed to provide good adhesion for the paint that will be added. You must be careful to not sand through the clear coat into the color, or this becomes a repair job, rather than one to enhance the existing paint.

Be sure to also use lots of water when scuffing the clear coat. This helps to float the loose particles away from the surface, instead of grinding them into the surface. Water can be applied by dipping the sandpaper into a bucket of water, or more easily by spraying on water from a squirt bottle.

This tank is for the same chopper and has already been scuffed to provide great adhesion. It has been dried and cleaned with wax and grease remover, as well. With the surface preparation complete and the filler neck taped off, Tim has roughed in the layout for a collection of skulls and bones.

Although the artwork is highly detailed at this point, it's nothing compared to what the final product will be. Airbrush work is very tedious and time consuming, and therefore expensive if you are paying to have it done. You can learn airbrush work by reading and practicing, but those lessons are beyond the scope of this book. Check out www.motorbooks.com for books on airbrush techniques.

Against the dark blue base of the tank, most of the artwork for this particular chopper is done in light blue, rather than white. If white paint had been used, the contrast would be too stark, and it would not look as good.

Lots of patience and even more practice are necessary for performing this kind of work. A creative mind and loads of talent also come in handy.

No two skulls are exactly alike. While it may not be readily apparent in the photos, there is a reptile of some sort slithering in and around the bones and skulls. Also, note that the oil tank filler and connections are masked off to keep paint from getting in the threaded connections.

Throughout the painting of these pieces, Tim is quick to turn the piece or prop it up on something to keep it in a position where he is comfortable. You simply cannot do this kind of detail-oriented work if you are not comfortable.

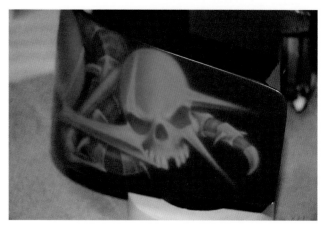

Perhaps this detail shot will provide some insight to Tim Kohl's airbrush talent. This is only the tip of the iceberg of creativity and talent in this young artist. Watch for more from Tim in the future.

SMOOTHING THE WELDS IN CUSTOM HANDLEBARS

Almost every chopper built these days sports a frame that looks as if it were made out of one piece of steel, with no welds to be seen when it is all finished. However, when you see that same frame or custom handlebars while they are still in raw metal form and before they have been smoothed, you will quickly understand that there are lots of welded joints on a chopper. Smoothing these welds before applying primer and paint sure makes the finished product look much better. It is not a difficult thing to do, but it takes some time. The process is the same, whether it's a bike frame, a set of handlebars, or other welded joints. To see how it's done, follow along as Donnie Karg at Karg's Hot Rod Service smoothes some handlebars.

This is what we started with, essentially four pieces of tubing. The two pieces of each handlebar were miter cut to give the desired shape when welded together. The fifth piece is a piece of smaller tubing that is welded in place to connect the two sides.

It should be obvious that if you are going to smooth the pieces, you must first smooth the weld itself. This will also test if your welds have sufficient penetration. If there are any gaps or structural weakening after you grind the weld smooth, the weld was not sufficient anyway, and needs to be redone.

This angle-head pneumatic grinder with a stick-on grinding disc works great for grinding objects that have limited access.

From a short distance away, these handlebars look pretty good as they are, although closer inspection will reveal some minor irregularities due to the grinding process. If you were not going to fill these minor low spots with some filler, you are probably better off to not grind the welds in the first place.

Occasionally, no grinder made will fit into some of the places that we would like for them to. In cases like this, you will need to use some 36- or 80-grit sandpaper to smooth down the weld bead.

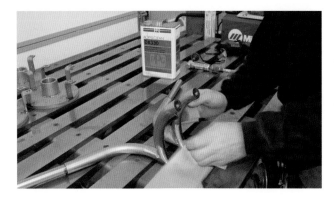

When the weld bead has been ground/sanded down sufficiently, wipe the parts with wax and grease remover to ensure proper adhesion of the body filler.

Wax and grease remover is sprayed on or wiped on with a clean towel, and then wiped off with another clean towel. Note the use of yet another towel for holding the handlebars to minimize the transfer of skin oil onto the work piece.

You can buy plastic filler mixing boards, or boards with tear-off sheets, but if you are going to be mixing a small amount of plastic body filler, a piece of cardboard will work just as well. Mix the desired amount of filler with a proportionate amount of hardener until the color is uniform throughout. It can be something of a guessing game; most likely, you will mix too much or too little.

If the surface to be filled were larger or flatter, common practice would be to apply the filler with a flat, flexible spreader. However, on tubular surfaces such as handlebars or chopper frames, you may need to apply the filler by hand. Disposable gloves help to keep skin oil from contaminating and spoiling the filler, plus their use makes for easier cleanup when the job is completed.

If you are dealing with difficult-to-reach areas like this, make sure that you push the filler thoroughly into the gap, so that there is not a void between the filler and the part you are smoothing.

As long as the filler does not exceed 1/8 inch thick, you can apply it as thick as you want and don't need to worry about getting it uniform, as sanding will remove the excess.

After the filler has begun to "tack up," you can begin sanding it with 80- or 100-grit sandpaper. If the filler simply starts smearing around when you start sanding, you need to wait a little longer. If you start making "dust" when you are sanding, you can get after it.

Start by sanding off the obvious high spots and globs of filler. Then progress around the rest of the filled area until all of the tacky outer surface has been sanded away.

After the entire filled area has been sanded with 80- or 100-grit sandpaper, you can switch to 200- or 220-grit sandpaper to remove the scratches left from the coarse paper.

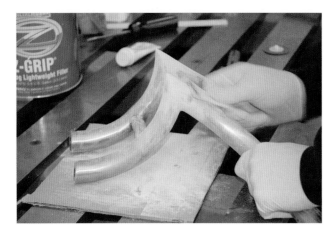

The gray spots are the high spots where there is no filler. The light blue/green shows where there is a very thin coat of filler remaining.

Now that the low spots have all been filled, only a few sanding scratches remain to be filled. At this point, switch over to a glazing type of filler that has a finer consistency. It is mixed with the same type of hardener as the previous filler until the color is uniform throughout.

Again, the filler is applied by wiping it on by hand for this particular application. Apply a thin layer over the entire area that has been filled.

It won't take long for this filler to dry to the point of being work-able, since it is so thin, but you do need to give it time to dry com-pletely. Since the layer is so thin, if you begin working it too soon, you will be losing ground, rather than speeding the process.

Use 320-grit sandpaper to initially sand this finer glazing filler. When all of the excess filler has been removed, switch to 400-grit sandpaper to sand away any scratches remaining from the coarser grits of sandpaper.

Be sure to take your time and work the nooks and crannies to the same point of perfection as the rest of the part. One bad area, no matter how small, can spoil the whole illusion.

After thorough sanding, use an air nozzle to blow away any sand-ing dust, and look for any areas that may still need work. If you find low spots, fill them now with more glazing filler.

Left: When it appears that no additional filler is required and the sanding is complete, clean the part with wax and grease remover. Hang the part from a suitable fixture (an engine stand in this case), and then apply the primer of your choice. After the primer dries, inspect the parts for areas that need more filler or sanding prior to painting.

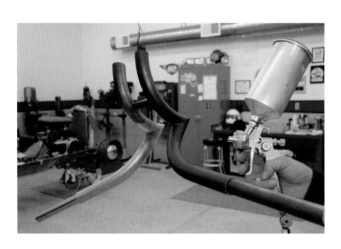

PAINTING A CHOPPER GAS TANK

Although we don't like to think about it, a reality of riding any type of motorcycle is that you may lay it down on occasion for any of a number of reasons. When this happens, besides yourself and your passenger, the gas tank is often the recipient of much of the road rash. You may not have the time or talent to re-create the artwork that was on your chopper, but you can probably paint the tank sufficiently to get the bike back on the road. Let's face it, if riding season is just dawning in your particular part of the world, you may not want to put your bike in the shop just now . . . especially if it has been a long winter of no riding.

Whether the tank is a new replacement, a used replacement, or the one that was involved in the mishap, as long as it can be repaired (read that as NO leaks), it can be repainted. Tim Kohl gives us the quick lowdown on repainting a gas tank.

Damage to this tank was only on the left side and was limited to minor dents and scratches. Tim has already mixed and applied a skim coat of plastic body filler to fill the low spots. The filler has already been rough sanded with 100-grit and then 220-grit sandpaper.

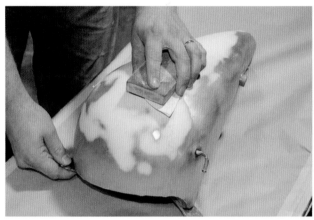

Tim uses 400-grit sandpaper on a sanding block to final sand the tank in preparation for primer.

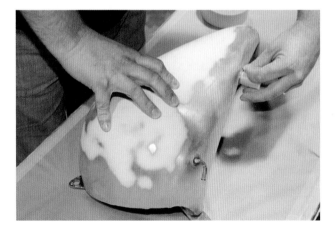

Tank fittings are then masked off with 1 1/2-inch-wide masking tape.

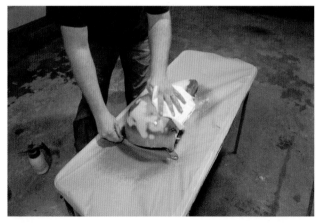

Next, Tim uses a clean paper towel that has been moistened with wax and grease remover to remove any oil, grease, wax, or other contaminants. Use a clean paper towel to then wipe off any excess wax and grease remover.

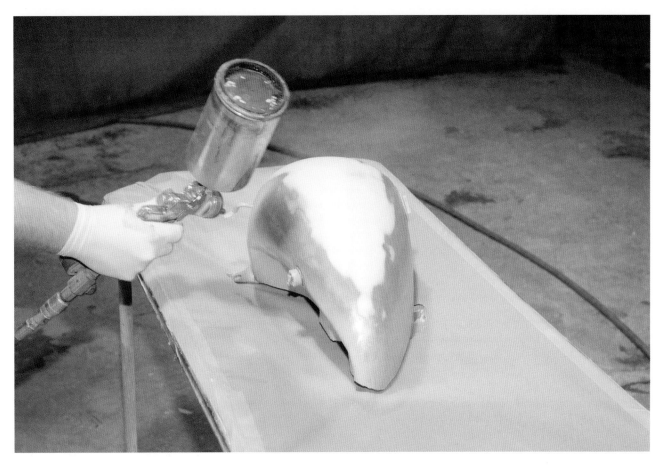

The next step is to mix up a small amount of epoxy primer with the appropriate catalyst. Be sure to check the manufacturer's recommendations for spray gun pressure, the number of coats required, and the drying time between coats. Then apply the epoxy primer to the tank.

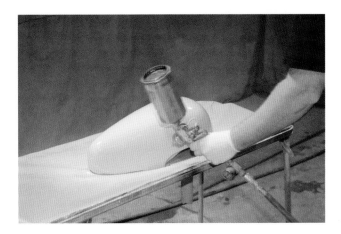

After the recommended drying time, apply the second (and successive) coats as required.

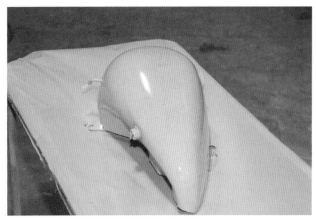

After the recommended flash dry time, Tim mists on some contrasting color paint from a spray can to form a guide coat. This guide coat is the small gray specks seen most abundantly in the middle of the tank.

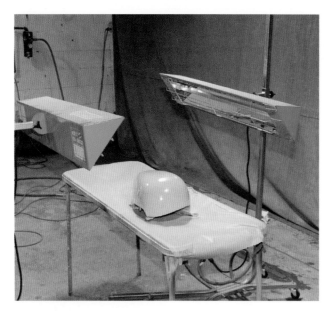

To speed the drying time between primer and paint, Tim uses a pair of infrared heaters. What would have taken nearly 2 hours at ambient room temperature was reduced to less than 30 minutes by using the heaters.

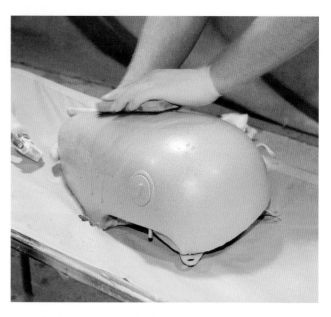

Since this is epoxy primer, it can be wet sanded. Tim uses 800-grit sandpaper and sands in an "X" pattern to obtain a flat surface.

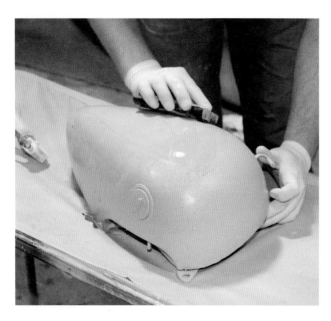

When the gray specks of the guide coat are sanded off, the surface should be uniform, and therefore ready to paint.

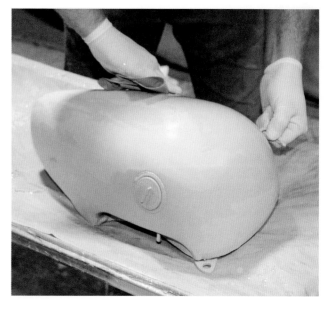

Again, Tim uses wax and grease remover to clean the surface.

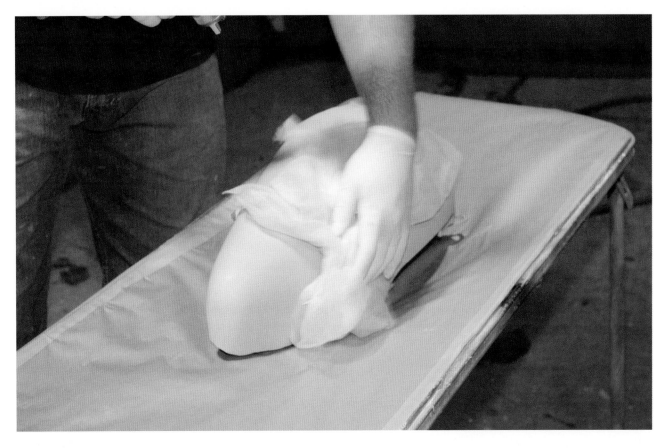

Be sure to dry off any excess wax and grease remover with a second, clean, dry paper towel.

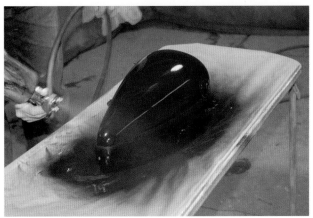

Consult the manufacturer's recommendations for the correct mixing ratio and spray gun pressure. Apply the color of your choice. The paint will look glossy since it is still wet, but will be dull in appearance if you are using base coat/clear coat.

Just as between primer and paint, allow the appropriate drying times (using heaters, if required). Then apply clear coat according to the manufacturer's recommendations.

DIFFERENT TYPES OF PAINT AND EFFECTS

Paint and painting effects are limited only by the imagination (and skill) of the painter and perhaps to a certain extent by the presence (or lack thereof) of someone to pay to do the work. Showcasing all of the paint treatments that have been used over the years would fill an entire book . . . and that is if you used only the examples of good artwork. Showing examples of less than pleasing results or lack of detail could fill libraries.

Above: These flames are very traditional in layout, and in this case exhibit a simple two-color combination. Silver flames on a purple base are outlined by a lavender pinstripe. More elaborate flames would typically fade from one of three or four colors throughout the length of the flame. Whether the flames are one color or several, traditional flames need to have a pinstripe outline to look their best.

These flames use very short licks, even though the flames extend most of the length of the vehicle. Although the coloring is very similar to the rest of the car with a strong outline airbrushed in, they should not be confused with ghost flames or outline flames.

Yellow flames just seem to jump off the red paint on this red coupe. Notice how the yellow color extends from the front to about halfway through the lick and then becomes more of an outline flame in a short transition. Whether you like it or not is up to you; this is merely one type of flame layout.

Notice how these flames have color the entire length with some slight fading around the edges. Also the very front of the flames (around the grille shell) start out as white and then blend into yellow.

As if the airbrushed layout wasn't wild enough, various colors and shades of candy colors give this chopper much visual impact.

The rear fender of this chopper provides a better look at the tribal flames, which appear to be three-dimensional atop the candy colors. Obviously, they aren't three-dimensional . . . or are they?

No one says graphics on a chopper have to be colorful. These camouflage graphics would require quite a bit of work to reproduce.

Although some guys might be offended by the flowers on this bike, it would be appropriate for a woman's chopper or someone who spends a lot of time cruisin' Margaritaville.

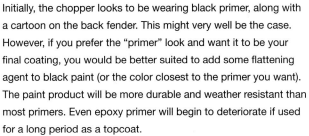

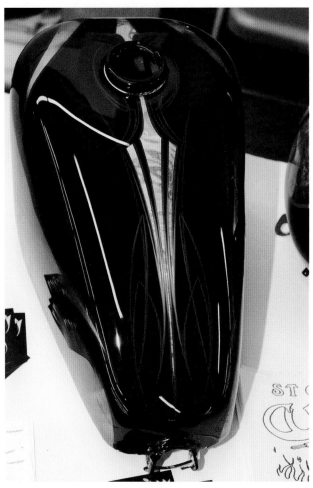

Initially, the chopper looks to be wearing black primer, along with a cartoon on the back fender. This might very well be the case. However, if you prefer the "primer" look and want it to be your final coating, you would be better suited to add some flattening agent to black paint (or the color closest to the primer you want). The paint product will be more durable and weather resistant than most primers. Even epoxy primer will begin to deteriorate if used for a long period as a topcoat.

We don't know what the rest of the bike will look like, but if this tank is any indication, it should look very nice. Subtle perhaps, but very nice. Supersmooth black paint, accented with freehand pinstriping is enhanced by the addition of some gold leaf.

These flames are a combination of realistic flames, which are becoming very popular, and tribal flames. The coloring and faded edges provide the realistic look, while the shape is purely tribal.

Above: These flames look more realistic than the previous example. Again, the edges of the red/orange that would indicate a particular degree of heat are realistically soft. The inner edges of the yellow are a bit sharper, although not crisp, resulting in very realistic-looking flames.

Right: Close inspection will show metal flake paint both as a base color and also repeated in some of the hot licks. Several layers of flames can be found on this wild chopper.

Some people will call these scallops while others may call them lightening bolts. No matter what you call them, they are easy for the beginning painter to apply. Since the edges are all straight (albeit skewed), they can be masked off easily. Determining which colors to use is perhaps the most difficult part of the task. As with traditional flames, be sure to finish the edges with a thin pinstripe.

This Model A sedan features a different twist on scallops. First of all, the lower side of each scallop is curved, making consistency very important and masking more difficult. Additionally, each curved scallop has an inset of another color that matches the color of the grille shell.

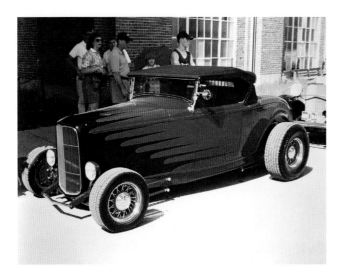

The black scallops make a stark contrast to the red paint on the roadster. Notice the precision in the layout of the scallops. The tops are all parallel, the bottoms are all parallel, and the round bellies all fall along a straight (albeit slanted) line.

This early chopper reeks of nostalgia with its springer front end, chain drive, and whitewalls. Satin black primer (flattened black paint) is highlighted by some traditional scallops.

These scallops work very well on this chopper with its fabricated gas tank. The lines of the scallops blend nicely with the lines of the tank, and they would be easy to lay out.

CHAPTER 4
POWDER COATING

An alternative to paint for adding color is having the parts powder coated. This process is particularly suited to vehicles that are driven often, as powder coating provides a tough and durable finish that is easy to maintain. However, contrary to popular belief, powder coating is not 100 percent impervious to damage. It is most vulnerable to impact damage, but if you impact your chopper or hot rod, chances are that you are gonna do more damage somewhere else anyway.

What Is Powder Coating?

For all intents and purposes, powder coating is simply a different process for applying paint. The various resins, pigments, and other components that are combined to make up the powder are first mixed together and then partially cured, converting into a solid. This solid material is then ground into fine powder, hence the name. All of the work to this point is performed by the manufacturer of the powder.

As long as the curing process doesn't heat the cylinder heads to the point of damaging them, powder coating is a good way to add color to the engine. Although it would require extra effort on the part of the person spraying the powder, an additional step toward detailing would be to wipe the powder off the edges of the fins prior to curing. The fins could then be left natural or polished.

For automotive applications, powder coating's main advantages are excellent UV resistance and very good resistance to harmful chemicals and corrosion. To achieve these properties, powder coating resins should be acrylic, urethane, polyester, or TGIC polyester. The components that provide resistance to UV rays are what provide the excellent gloss for which powder coating is known. Other resins are available for other purposes, but are not suitable for road-going applications.

Powder is then sprayed with a powder coating gun onto suspended parts from which static electricity draws the powder. After being completely coated with the colored powder, the parts are moved into an oven. The parts are then baked, causing the powder to melt into a continuous film and then cure.

To improve the durability of powder coating, a coat of clear powder can be applied after the color coat, using the same process.

Pros/Cons

Like almost anything, there are pros and cons to powder coating. In the case of powder coating, the disadvantages are fairly limited and are usually outweighed by the advantages.

Pros

The continuous film that powder melts into is the main reason for its corrosion resistance. As solvents escape from liquid paint during the drying process, the solvents leave microscopic pinholes. These pinholes are extremely tiny and would have to be magnified several times to be seen. However, they still provide an entrance for moisture and chemicals to work their way beneath that freshly painted surface.

Unlike many liquid paint products, the materials used in powder coating are environmentally friendly. Note that while safety precautions must be followed during the coating process, the materials used are less harmful to the environment and can be recycled. Although solvents are used in the production of the powder itself, none are added during the use of the product by the end user; therefore, very low emissions of harmful chemicals exist during the curing process. Another benefit is that the VOC (volatile organic compound) rating is typically less than 1 pound per gallon for powder, while the VOC rating for automotive paint is typically between 2.5 and 7 pounds per gallon.

Additionally, powder overspray can be collected and reused, presuming of course that you are spraying in an area that is not contaminated by other chemicals. Overspray from liquid paint is completely useless and must be disposed of.

Cons

Items to be powder coated must be able to withstand temperatures up to around 450 degrees Fahrenheit for up to 30 minutes. Some parts simply cannot be powder coated for this very reason. Fiberglass components such as fenders are an obvious example of this. With exact color matching between paint and powder coating being a trial-and-error process at best, painted fenders and their close proximity to a powder-coated frame may result in a less than desired outcome.

Curing powder coating material requires an oven or infrared lamps. Larger ovens designed just for powder coating or pottery kilns are available, but they start getting real expensive in a hurry when you begin looking at price tags. You would need to have several chopper frames or hot rod chassis lined up and ready to be coated to justify the expense of an oven large enough to accommodate them. However, for small parts, a discarded toaster oven will suffice, while the oven from a kitchen stove will work for most of the larger parts associated with a chopper. *An important note: Do not use any oven for food preparation after it has been used to cure powder coating!* Infrared lamps are somewhat expensive and are not enclosed, so you are essentially heating the entire area where they are located. However, with many parts being relatively small, the infrared lamps can be placed very close to the parts they are to cure. These lamps can also be used with traditional paint products, so with their versatility they may not be beyond a justifiable expense.

What Can/Cannot Be Powder Coated

As long as the part is metal and can withstand the temperature required to cure the powder (usually between 350 and 450 degrees Fahrenheit), it can probably be powder coated. Powder coating cannot be applied over any type of plastic body filler.

The inability to withstand the heat rules out plastic parts. Rumors abound over the development of powders that are designed to cure at low temperatures, however those products are not commercially available at this time. Cylinder heads or other parts that would be ruined if they warped should not be powder coated. This is not to say that you couldn't have a nonworking cylinder head powder coated for display purposes or for a lamp base, but the risk of warping is too great to apply this type of coating to a functional engine part.

Surface Preparation

Metal surfaces to be powder coated must be stripped to the bare metal and free of grease, oils, or any other contaminants. Even parts that have been coated with primer must be stripped to bare metal. Most commercial facilities that do powder coating have the necessary equipment to get down to the bare metal or they work closely with a subcontractor who does. Powder coating and stripping to bare metal go hand in hand, so except in very rare instances, you should be able to take your parts to a reputable powder coater and they can take care of the entire process for you.

Cleaning

Whether you do it yourself or pay someone else to do the work, the parts to be prepped for powder coating need to be sorted by metal type, such as steel, aluminum, or zinc, so that they can be cleaned properly. If the parts do not have any paint, chrome, or other finishes on them, they can simply be cleaned and then coated. Steel parts should be cleaned with an alkaline type cleaner, while other types of metal must be cleaned with milder cleaners such as Simple Green or Fast Orange.

Paint Stripper

Steel parts and some other metals can be stripped of old paint with paint stripper. This type of product may not be suitable for use on all metals or finishes, so you should consult your paint supply jobber for their recommendations on which products to use.

When using paint stripper, be sure to follow all safety precautions on the label of the product, as it is some nasty stuff. As someone who has stripped a complete pickup truck by hand with paint stripper, I strongly recommend that you wear a respirator, thick shoes or boots, long pants, and long-sleeved shirt. If you were to happen to drop a glob of paint stripper on some bare skin, you would quickly wish that you hadn't. Fortunately, it only burns for a while . . .

The one thing that the instructions for paint stripper don't tell you is that you should scuff the painted surface prior to applying paint stripper. If you are dealing with decently applied paint, it becomes a Mexican standoff between the paint and the stripper. You will do yourself a favor and use less stripper if you scuff the surface with sandpaper beforehand to allow the stripper to more easily penetrate the surface. Although I would not attempt to strip a complete car or truck by hand ever again, any one part is considerably smaller, and therefore less involved.

Media Blasting

If you are prepping parts that are not suitable for stripping via paint stripper, the parts may be media blasted. This is a great way to remove paint, peeling chrome, and rust, plus it is a great way to induce adhesion of the powder coating. However, you cannot simply start blasting away at your parts.

Three very important things to remember when media blasting are 1) mask the area that should not be blasted, 2) use the appropriate blasting media, and 3) remove all of the blasting media when the job is complete. You must also wear proper safety apparel, including eye and respiratory protection.

Masking

No matter what type of media is being used, media blasting will leave a textured surface. For this reason, machined surfaces, bearing surfaces, or threaded areas should be masked from media blasting. Exterior threads can be easily protected from blasting by covering them with a length of appropriately sized rubber hose or tubing. Other areas can be masked with heavy cardboard and masking tape, accompanied by prudent use of lower blasting pressure and a careful aim.

Media Selection

Media used for blasting needs to be compatible with the material upon which it is being used. If the blasting media

BLAST MEDIA	SURFACE MATERIAL	TYPE OF BLASTING	RECOMMENDED AIR PRESSURE (PSI)
Glass Bead	Aluminum, brass, die casts	Cleaning	60
Aluminum Oxide	Steel	Removing rust and paint; increasing adhesion of paint or powder coating	80–90
Silicon Carbide	Steel	Preparation for welding	80–90
Walnut Shells	Engine/transmission assemblies	Cleaning	80
Plastic Media	Sheet metal	Removing paint	30–90
Aluminum Shot	Aluminum, brass, die cast	Cleaning	80–90

is harder than the surface being prepped, you will do more harm than good by hurling millions of tiny, hard objects at it. A large volume of softer media passing by the surface is a more appropriate way of freeing the surface of unwanted material. These softer materials typically include silica sand, aluminum oxide, plastic media, or walnut shells. You should avoid using steel shot media or coarse river sand.

For a long time, common river sand was used extensively for media blasting, hence the now-outdated term of sand blasting. Sand can be and is still used to remove graffiti and for surface preparation for steel bridges, masonry structures, and various other applications. However, sand can quickly put heavy scratches into something as relatively light as a chopper frame. It also causes significant heat, which will quickly warp sheetmetal panels.

Silica sand is much finer than river sand, although it has drawbacks as well. Using any kind of sand for blasting purposes will create an extremely fine dust, which is known to cause the human ailment silicosis. This extremely nasty side effect can be avoided by using any of a number of alternative products.

Various materials other than sand are available for use in media blasting and tumbling processes. No one material is the best for all cleanup operations, so be sure to match the media with the task. At the lower end of the price scale are glass beads, aluminum oxide, and walnut shells. Walnut shells are the best choice for cleaning grease, oil, and other residue from transmissions and engines. For remov-

ing paint and rust from steel, aluminum oxide is the best choice. Although it is not the best media for any particular cleanup project, glass bead blasting does a good job on almost any surface. Silicon carbide is about twice the cost of these media, but will typically do a better job and is ideal for cleaning surfaces prior to welding. A little more expensive is plastic media, which is best for stripping paint from metal, as it doesn't get as hot and cause warping. Aluminum shot is best for cleaning soft metals such as aluminum, die casts, and brass, although it is more expensive.

The following chart gives media and air pressure setting recommendations for various blasting projects.

When choosing a blasting media, you must remember that any scratches or abrasions that you put into the metal while cleaning it will also need to be taken out. An aggressive media will no doubt remove paint and other finishes faster, but if the media is harder than the material being blasted, you will get to a point where you are creating more work for yourself.

Media Removal

In addition to the flaking rust, paint, or whatever was on the part prior to blasting, you must also remove all of the blasting media when the blasting is finished. Much of the media used for blasting is recycled and used again, so even if your parts were not oily or greasy, previously blasted parts may have been. Any oil that is present on the parts will be pushed deeper into the surface during the baking process, so it is imperative that all parts be cleaned thoroughly after being media blasted.

Burnoff Cleaning

Some powder coating shops use ovens to heat parts to up around 900 degrees Fahrenheit to remove previous finishes. This high heat will break down the bonding agents of most finishes, and then the residue is removed with high-pressure washing. Aluminum products **cannot** be cleaned this way, as aluminum simply cannot withstand the high heat without losing its strength.

Applying Powder

For convenience in handling, most powder coaters hang their parts with a wire from a movable rack. Being suspended in the air allows unlimited access to the part to ensure complete coverage. With the parts to be coated grounded and the powder coating gun electrically charged, the powder is applied to the parts using low-velocity air. The powder is held in place by static electricity. After applying the powder, the parts rack with the coated parts is moved into the curing area. You must exercise care when moving the parts so that no powder is inadvertently knocked off.

In addition to its durability benefits, powder coating is appealing to many because it is easy to apply. After the part to be coated is cleaned, the powder is simply sprayed on until the entire part is covered. You will want to get the powder applied relatively evenly, but by the very nature of the process, the coating will typically even itself out as it is heated and when curing. This eliminates much of the stress that some hobbyists incur with the painting process, where too much or too little paint may cause problems.

However, powder coating is thicker than typical paint, so you must avoid using the more-is-better philosophy, especially in areas where certain part clearances must be kept (such as a motorcycle swingarm and its related bushings) or where the engine mounts to the frame. An abundance of powder coating in these stressed areas is susceptible to being crushed and eroded away, causing bolts to loosen slightly in the process. Verifying the correct torque in these critical areas at regular intervals on a freshly completed hot rod or chopper would be a good suggestion, no matter what type of finish is applied.

Masking

For masking any areas that should not be powder coated, high temperature plugs (of various sizes) and high temperature tape (in various widths) can be used. These products are available wherever you purchase your coating supplies.

Another method for masking is to actually apply powder to the entire part, and then use a fine-tipped air nozzle to blow the powder away from areas that are not to be coated. You do have to be very careful that you remove all of the powder from any areas that are not to be coated.

Curing

The temperature of the oven and the length of time required for curing will vary, depending on the powder coating resin that is being cured. Varying the time and the temperature in the curing oven will alter such characteristics as color holdout, gloss retention, and hardness (durability). For these reasons, you should follow the recommendations of the powder manufacturer for the particular powder that you are using.

A curing time of 15 to 20 minutes at a temperature of 350 to 400 degrees Fahrenheit is fairly common. After the appropriate length of time, the cured parts should be removed from the curing oven and allowed to cool. They should be allowed to continue hanging for as long as possible to allow full airflow around the part to cool it uniformly. Whenever the parts are cool enough to handle, they can be returned to service, making this a relatively quick process.

Clear Powder Coating

To improve the durability of powder coating, as well as add depth and luster, a coat of clear powder can be applied after the color coat. The clear powder is applied after the color coat has been cured, but while the piece is still hot. Pieces and parts that have been given a clear coat are returned to the curing oven for a second curing process.

Sometimes referred to as poor man's chrome, clear powder coating by itself can be applied to metal parts that have been polished to a high luster.

Getting Started

If you are dealing with new parts or parts that don't require more than minor cleaning for preparation, doing your own powder coating is an easy process to get into. The equipment needed is readily available and reasonably priced from a variety of sources. However, except for an air supply (air compressor), most of the equipment is job specific. In other words, you aren't going to use a powder coating gun for anything other than powder coating, so you should qualify your purchase and shop accordingly.

Necessary Equipment

Other than the time required to actually do the work and the money for purchasing the equipment, the list of necessities for doing your own powder coating is a short list. These equipment requirements are a powder coating gun, a curing oven, a source of compressed air, electricity, powder coating powder, and a few minor expendable items. Those first two items are sometimes the most difficult to obtain.

Powder Coating Gun

Powder coating guns range in price from just under $100 for a hobbyist quality unit to professional units that cost close to $3,000. There are at least a couple of stops between these two extremes, so do some shopping before you plunk down the long, hard green.

The noticeable difference between the types of guns (besides their respective prices) is the amount of powder that they can dispense before you have to reload or refill the powder cup. If you are going to be doing small groups of small parts, a hobbyist gun will work fine. If you foresee coating a large number of small parts at any one time or a few large parts, you may need to opt for a larger gun to avoid the need to refill the gun in the middle of a production run. If you are planning to start a business where the bulk of your business will be large quantities of anything, large or small, you should take the plunge and purchase a larger gun from the beginning. It should be obvious that you will need to change powder material any time that you wish to change colors.

Curing Oven

This is what really limits the size of the pieces and parts that you can powder coat. If the coated part won't fit into the curing oven, it can't be cured. However, portable infrared lamps allow you to avoid the oven size restriction.

Ovens designed especially for powder coating can easily cost over $8,000 and quickly go upward from there, which would realistically limit their use to small coating businesses. Infrared lamps (that can also be used for speeding the drying time of paint) can be purchased for a few hundred dollars. Although larger projects may require more lamps, their smaller individual price and versatility seems to make this a more realistic method of meeting the requirements.

Air Supply

A very small powder coating job could make do with an air tank that is equipped with a regulator so airflow can be adjusted. An air compressor that is capable of producing additional air is a more viable alternative than loading the air tank in the truck and taking it to the corner gas station every time you need a refill. An air compressor with a larger tank will also allow you to coat more parts at one time without being required to stop to allow the compressor to catch up.

Electric Source

Lower-priced coating guns are available in 120-volt models, so their use should not pose any problems in your home shop. Larger guns may require additional electric service, so you should verify the electric requirements of the equipment that you plan to use if you are considering powder coating as a business. If you are going into business, be sure to consult your local authorities for regulations and requirements regarding permits, wiring, zoning, and anything else that may cause problems to the uninformed.

Powder

Powder used for powder coating is available from a variety of sources. Most suppliers refer to standard colors, specialty colors, and custom colors, or some variation thereof. Standard colors are just that, and they include most basic colors, along with those that match engine colors of some automobiles. Specialty colors are typically more exotic or feature minor special effects such as candies or metallics. Custom colors include those that resemble chrome, iridescent paint, or other special effects.

Standard colors are the least expensive, while the custom colors are the most expensive. Powders are available in different quantities, making it possible to purchase as much or as little as you need with minimal waste. Standard powders are even more economical when purchased in larger quantities, although the amount of savings drops somewhat in relation to the overall expense when buying custom products in bulk. If you will need the larger quantity of the custom material, it is less expensive to purchase it at one time, but that does not mean it will be cheap.

Other Necessities

Expendable items that you will need are various types of masking material and wire for hanging parts. High-temperature fiberglass tape can be used for masking external threads and machined surfaces. Silicon plugs in different sizes are used for plugging holes that need to be masked from powder coating material.

Environmental Issues

Although the process for making powder involves various solvents that contain VOCs, the chemical companies are saddled with those responsibilities. Once the powder is created by the chemical company, no additional solvents—and therefore no VOCs—are emitted, making this an environmentally friendly finish process. You should still wear appropriate safety equipment such as a paint suit and respirator, but this should be done at any time chemicals are being used.

To see the powder coating process in person, Ron Leadford at C.R. Metal Products took me on a quick tour of their paint line. Although painting in the common sense of the term is different from powder coating, powder coating is simply a different method of applying paint. Even though the parts being coated at the time were not for use on a chopper or hot rod, they do show the various steps in the process.

In this commercial powder coating facility, most of the work is automated to provide consistent results and lower labor costs. The first step is to hang the parts to be powder coated on a continually moving overhead conveyor. Although powder will be applied by another person, this is the last time that the parts will be touched by human hands until after they are cured.

Upon closer inspection, we see that nylon plugs have been inserted into the threaded holes to mask them from receiving powder.

Wire hangers are uniformly suspended from the overhead conveyor chain. From these, flat steel hangers that are designed for various products are hung. These can hold a number of items, depending on their size and shape.

After being hung on the powder coating line, the parts first go into an automated cleaning system. The diagonally oriented strips are flexible, which allows parts of various sizes to go through the cleansing system.

Fans and heaters located inside of the cleaning section help to dry the parts. From here, the parts will meander along their way to where the powder will be applied. More fans and heaters will dry the parts, and once finished the parts will travel to the powder room.

While these parts are obviously larger than the ones we've seen so far, the conveyor does not stop. Proper spacing of the parts on the conveyor allows the process to continue nonstop. The opening on the opposite wall is the inlet of a filtered vacuum system, which sucks up excess powder. Because of the excess powder, proper safety equipment (namely a respirator) is a necessity.

These pieces have received powder on both sides and are moving toward the oven for curing. These particular parts will cook for about 20 minutes at a temperature of around 400 degrees Fahrenheit.

Finished pieces come out of the oven with a very durable surface. At the end of the line, they can be removed from the conveyor. After quality inspection, they go directly into their packaging.

CHAPTER 5
POLISHING

Whether you are going to polish a piece of metal and leave it that way, or if you plan to plate it, anodize it, or chrome it, polishing is the process that determines the overall quality and appearance of the finished piece. Simply put, polishing is the process of smoothing an object by applying friction. Just as continuously rubbing a piece of sandpaper over a piece of wood will make it smooth, rubbing abrasive material over metal will make the metal smooth. The difference between wood and metal is that the metal has reflective qualities that are not present in wood.

What is actually being done during the polishing process is removal of microscopic surface imperfections. When a painter block sands the surface to be painted prior to applying paint, he is removing surface imperfections, so that the surface will be as perfect as possible. This perfect surface, based in no small part on the crystalline properties of metallic elements, is what provides the mirrorlike shine.

How It's Done

Polishing is done by first cleaning the part and removing any unwanted finishes, such as wax, grease, paint, or plating. After getting to the clean, bare metal, the part is sanded with increasingly finer grits of sanding material to remove scratches or other imperfections that can be felt or seen by eye. Then the part is polished with buffing compound (determined by the type of material) until the desired surface finish is obtained.

When the desired amount of "perfection" is obtained, the polished part can be enhanced by applying the finish of your choice, or simply left as is. These additional finishes include chrome or one of several other plating processes, powder coating, anodizing if the part is aluminum, or a coat of clear paint. For a polished part to be left "as is" and still retain good looks, it must first be made of a material that will not oxidize or rust (such as aluminum, stainless steel, or titanium), and it should then be coated with a wax or polishing product to minimize scratches or other environmental damage.

Necessary Equipment

The polishing process can be fairly easy or it can be labor intensive, a fact that is determined mainly by the equipment that you have available. Metals can be polished completely by hand without the use of any equipment (other than the polishing media itself). As you can imagine, depending on the size and shape of the part, this can be a time-consuming process, and it can even take a toll on your body physically if you are not careful. The process can be sped up considerably through the purchase of readily available equipment, which moves the pain from your shoulder and arms to your wallet.

Surface Cleaners

Before polishing any material, it must be clean and free of any wax, grease, or other contaminants that might spoil the finish. If the metal appears to be clean, it can be cleaned sufficiently by spraying or wiping on wax and grease remover, and then by thoroughly wiping that off with a clean towel. For metal that is obviously dirty, it should first be scrubbed with a soft bristle brush with soap and water, dried, and then cleaned with wax and grease remover as described above.

If the metal has been painted, powder coated, or plated, the surface will need to be removed by either chemical stripping or media blasting. Chemical stripping is an ideal method for cleaning sheetmetal parts as an inexperienced operator of media blasting equipment can quickly do more harm than good on relatively thin sheetmetal parts. Chemical stripping is also more suitable for larger parts. Most chopper parts are castings or forgings that are relatively small and usually beefier than sheet metal, so media blasting is more suitable for cleaning them. Chassis components for hot rods are usually hefty enough for media blasting also.

Blasting Cabinets

In its simplest form, a blasting cabinet can be described as an enclosed box that contains a pressurized air nozzle through which blasting media is sprayed at an object. The object is maneuvered by way of access holes for your hands in the front or side of the cabinet. A transparent panel in the front or top of the cabinet allows the operator to see what is being done inside the cabinet.

An air compressor is used to push the blasting media through the nozzle with sufficient force to remove previous finishes. The type of finish and the material being cleaned will determine which type of media should be used. See Chapter 4 for greater detail of blasting media types. When purchasing an air compressor to be used for media blasting, do yourself a favor and choose an air compressor that provides more pressure and volume than you think you need. Too little pressure is the common cause for less than desirable results when media blasting.

Two access holes in the front or side of the cabinet have "gloves" made of rubber or other suitable material attached to the inside of each access hole. These "gloves" provide protection for your arms and hands from the blasting media that is being forced through the air on the inside of the cabinet.

A feature of better blasting cabinets is an integral dust collector, although a separate shop vacuum can be used. Most commercially available blasting cabinets are designed like a hopper so that blasting material automatically flows to an access, where it can be dumped into a container, strained, and reused.

The benefit of a blasting cabinet is also its drawback. Being an enclosed cabinet, most of the blasting material is contained inside the unit. However, this cabinet design limits the size of anything that can be blasted. Having a portion of the part protruding through the access door would cause air pressure to quickly blow blasting media all over your workshop.

Small cabinets with a working capacity of about 2x2x3 feet can be purchased for around $300. Larger cabinets that will hold objects approximately 5 feet long are available in the $1,500–$2,000 range. Several cabinets of intermediate sizes are available and priced accordingly.

Portable Pressure Blasters

Pressure blasters are used more for industrial or automotive applications than for cleanup prior to polishing. However, they are worthy of mention as their use is justifiable and appropriate for cleaning a chopper frame or automobile chassis. Blasting media is poured into a sealable hopper that feeds into an outlet in the bottom of the hopper. Pressurized air (again from an air compressor) pushes the blasting media through a hose and handheld nozzle to remove existing finishes from the parts being blasted. Typically, a deadman valve is used on the nozzle, so that when the nozzle is released, airflow stops.

A portable pressure blaster will allow you to blast parts of unlimited size, although great effort must be taken to capture the blasting media for cleanup or to recycle. Even if merely for temporary use, a simple blasting area constructed of wooden 2x4s and plastic tarps or plywood could become a sizable cabinet to contain the media somewhat.

This type of equipment ranges in price from a few hundred dollars to around a thousand. For the truly budget minded, kits are available that provide a blasting gun that connects to your air supply and siphons blast media out of a bucket. Having adequate air pressure and dry media is a must with this type of system.

Whether you are using a blasting cabinet, a pressure blaster, or siphoning from a bucket, you should wear a respirator to minimize the intake of blasting media (and blasted surface) into your lungs. Even though a blasting cabinet will contain most of the media that is being used, most of that media is very, very fine, which allows some of it to escape. Whenever using a pressure blaster, you should wear a blast hood, long pants, a long-sleeved shirt, and heavy boots to protect your body from flying media.

Tumblers

If you need to de-rust several small items, such as nuts and bolts, a vibratory tumbler is a great way to get the job done. Manufacturing companies have used tumblers for years to smooth off the rough edges on pieces of flame-cut parts. Tumblers use media similar to what is used when blasting, but without air pressure. This media is poured into the tumbler along with the parts to be de-rusted, deburred, or just cleaned up. The tumbler is closed, turned on, and then begins to vibrate or rotate, depending on the style of tumbler. The motion inside the tumbler causes the media to abrade the surface, cleaning it in the process. The media/tumbler action is analogous to that of waves and beach sand smoothing broken hunks of glass.

Buffers

Now that you have removed all of the previous finishes and cleaned off all of the contaminants, you need a good buffer. When choosing a buffer, you should choose the correct motor speed, wheel size, a suitable wheel extension, and a comfortable working height.

Most metals can be buffed at 3,400 to 3,800 rpm, while plastics will need to be buffed at about half that speed to avoid burning. Prior to purchasing a buffer, you should first determine if you will be using it mostly for metal or for plastics, and buy a buffer with the appropriate motor speed. Obviously, if you are using a buffer that is belt operated, multistep pulleys will solve the motor speed issue if you are working on varied materials. If you are limited to one motor speed, you can effectively increase or decrease the motor speed somewhat by changing wheel sizes. For any given motor speed, the outer buffing surface of a larger buffing wheel will be spinning faster than that of a smaller buffing wheel. To increase the speed, use a larger wheel. To decrease the speed, use a smaller wheel. Larger-diameter buffing wheels will speed the buffing process and reach farther into some recesses, but may

Whether you build your own buffer from a discarded electric motor and some pulleys, or buy a new one, plating and polishing requires a buffer of some sort. This 1/3-horsepower buff motor shown is from Eastwood and is affordably priced even for a hobbyist. If you plan to get serious about doing this type of work, you should probably save some money in the long run and purchase a slightly larger unit from the beginning.

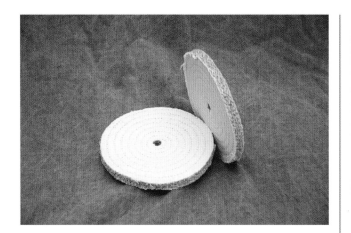

Spiral-sewn sisal wheels are the least flexible, and therefore the most aggressive of the buffing wheels. They are typically used for the first cutting action of a steel, iron, or stainless-steel work piece.

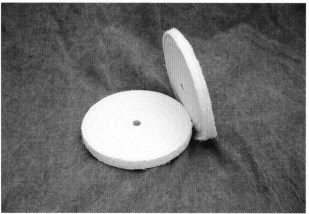

A spiral-sewn cotton wheel is more flexible than a sisal wheel, but is still relatively hard. It would be used for cutting actions in softer work pieces or to remove finer surface irregularities.

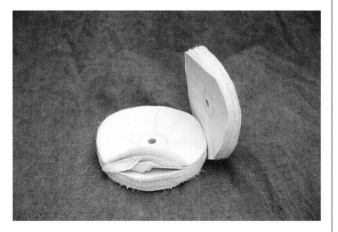

This photo shows that flap buffs are thin layers of material (cotton in this example) that are sewn together. This construction makes them very flexible for use in heavily contoured areas, and it helps to keep them running cool.

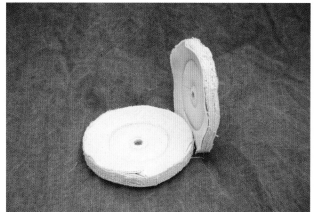

This cotton flannel buff is extremely soft, which makes it very good for bringing out the color in a polished work piece. It is also flexible, making it suitable for contoured areas.

not reach into confined areas. Refer to buffing accessories below for additional information on hard to reach areas.

Two variables that you may not consider at first are the amount of wheel extension that is necessary and a comfortable working height. The longer the shaft, the farther the buffing wheel is located away from the motor housing. This provides more maneuverability for reaching into the nooks and crannies of the parts you are buffing. A longer shaft also allows you to stack wheels to provide a wider buffing surface for doing larger, flatter areas at one time. If your buffer is pedestal mounted, an adjustable-height pedestal is a nice feature, as you can adjust it for standing, sitting on a

bar stool, or sitting in a chair. Whether pedestal-mounted or bench-mounted, the buffer should be set at a height that allows you to sit or stand up straight rather than crouched over. Bending over or crouching every time you use a buffer will lead to unnecessary back pain.

Buffing Wheels

Buffing wheels are available in a wide variety of styles and sizes, with each style serving a distinct purpose. In addition to matching the buffing wheel to the material that you will be using it on, you must also use a wheel with the appropriate-size center hole for the arbor of your buffer. Buffing wheels are available in sizes from around 4 to 10 inches in diameter.

Sisal wheels are commonly used for steel, iron, and stainless-steel surfaces. Fairly aggressive, they remove 400- to 500-grit sanding scratches, orange peel, or light casting marks. Sisal wheels are available covered with cotton, or for longer life, are available from the manufacturer with a treated surface that results in a more aggressive cutting of the metal's polished faces. Pleated sisal, for use on contoured surfaces, offers flexibility and cooler running.

Spiral-sewn wheels are made from cotton material that is sewn in a spiral. This spiral method of sewing the layers of cotton material together results in a hard wheel, making it a good choice for the cutting portion of polishing metal. Working well on all metals, spiral-sewn cotton removes 600-grit and finer scratches. Just as with sisal, treated spiral-sewn cotton wheels last longer and cut faster.

Ventilated flap buffs serve the same purpose as spiral-sewn wheels, but are designed for contoured surfaces. Multiple layers or flaps allow the wheel to flex more, reaching into contoured surfaces and keeping cooler at the same time. Like other wheels, treated versions cut faster and last longer.

Loose-section wheels are made of fine-weave cotton and are very flexible, which gives little cutting action, but brings out good color. These work well on hard or soft metals. Canton flannel wheels are made differently, but serve the same purpose as loose-section cotton wheels. Made from combed flannel, these wheels are very soft, and they provide the best shine on all metals, including gold and silver.

String wheels, usually made of cotton strands, are extremely flexible. These strings reach into deep areas and also minimize heating, making them ideal for polishing plastic surfaces, such as marker lights or taillight lenses.

Buffing Compound

In addition to a selection of buffing wheels, many different buffing compounds are available. Abrasive powders are added to a wax substance to make up buffing compounds. As the buffing compound is applied to the buffing wheel, generated heat causes the wax-based compound to melt onto the wheel. Compounds are available in tubes and in bars, and can be in a variety of colors. These different colors don't mean that the polished parts will be different colors when you are finished. It simply means that any one type of compound from one vendor may be a different color from that of another vendor.

Greaseless compounds are gritty material (in grits from 80 to 320), used to aggressively smooth out rough edges before polishing with other compounds.

Emery compound is used for coarse buffing to remove scratches and burrs from hard metals. Containing emery grit, it offers fast cutting action. *Stainless* compound offers fast cutting action on ferrous metals such as iron, steel, and stainless steel. *Tripoli* compound is used for general cutting on soft metals, such as aluminum and brass.

Other compounds are used for other materials or other uses. *Plastic* compound is used for removing scratches from plastic items, such as taillights. *Jeweler's rouge* is a very fine compound for use on gold, silver, or other precious metals. *White rouge* is used on metal to bring out the best color and mirrorlike finish in metal prior to plating.

Buffing Accessories

Wide varieties of accessories are available for varied buffing procedures. Quite often, these accessories can be used with a handheld drill or die grinder to eliminate the need for a typical buffer motor. By connecting a flexible shaft to an electric motor (consider salvaging the motor from that leaking washing machine before you throw it away!), you

The colors of compounds will vary from manufacturer to manufacturer. Compounds are also available in bars or in tubes as shown. When using tubes, the cardboard tubing is simply torn away as needed. Shown left to right, top to bottom are emery, stainless, white rouge, plastic, tripoli, and Jeweler's rouge.

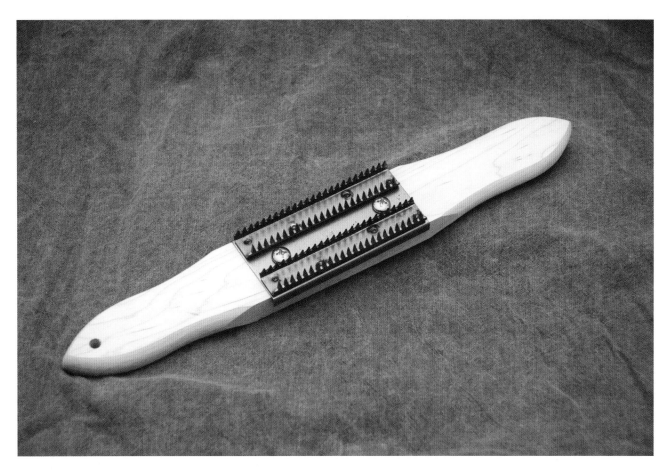

As excess compound dries on your buffing wheel, it will start to clog and begin having less than efficient results. To remove these drying clumps of compound, hold a buff rake at both ends and pass the serrated teeth over the buffing wheel momentarily.

can create a versatile buffing machine. With a small mandrel, miniature buffing wheels, and a roll-around cart, you can easily take the buffer to the part to be polished.

You will need a buff rake to clean dried buffing compound from the buffing wheel. Simply hold the buff rake against the spinning buffing wheel to clean the wheel. Just make sure you have a firm grip on the buffing rake to avoid launching it across the shop.

Buffing bobs are made of medium-density materials and designed to get into hard-to-reach areas. They are typically used with a mandrel in a handheld drill, or they can be mounted on the end of a flexible shaft that is attached to a motor. Buffing bobs come in a variety of shapes and sizes, typically made of a metal shaft with buffing material attached to the end. Felt bobs are similar, but are designed more for cutting than polishing in those hard to reach areas. Mushroom buffs, usually made of fine-weave cotton and extremely soft, allow you to polish intricate or highly contoured areas that are hard to reach.

Portable Buffers

Whether you call it a grinder, a sander, a buffer, or a polisher, one of these tools fitted with a buffing pad or a polishing bonnet is typically used to maintain the lustrous finish on paint or polished materials. You can achieve the same results by applying the polish or wax by hand, but why work harder than you have to? Just remember, you can burn through the paint or burn the plated finish much easier when a machine is doing the work.

Polishes/Waxes

Polishes and waxes for painted, polished, or plated materials are available at most auto parts stores or wherever you purchase your painting or plating supplies. They are available from a variety of manufacturers, and you'll have the choice of several similar products with many different names. Consult your local dealer for their specific recommendations.

Quick-cut cleaners remove scratches from color sanded painted surfaces. They should be used with a wool or foam pad at less than 1,800 rpm. Cleaner wax is used for removing scratches, stains, or oxidation from painted surfaces. It is typically applied with a foam pad at less than 1,800 rpm to avoid burning the paint.

Polishing Process

Almost any nonpolished surface would look like jagged mountains and valleys if magnified sufficiently. This uneven surface attempts to reflect light back at varied angles, which is what causes the surface to appear rough, as the light is actually being dissipated every which way rather than focused in one direction. If these rough surfaces are smoothed down, the object is able to reflect light better and become shinier (imagine the relatively calm surface of a mountain lake), even if all the surfaces are not on the same geometric plane. As the surfaces are smoothed even more and brought into the same plane, they become mirrorlike.

Cutting and Coloring (Polishing)

"Cutting" is the term for initially smoothing the surface by removing casting marks, scratches, and other blemishes. This is done by moving the work piece in the opposite direction to the buffing wheel's rotation (pulling the work piece toward you as the rotating buffing wheel moves away from you). When cutting, you should use a medium to hard pressure on the work piece. When finished with the cutting procedure, the surface should be smooth, semibright, and uniform in appearance.

"Coloring" is what provides the bright, shiny, and clean surface. To achieve the best color, the work piece is moved in the same direction as the rotating buffing wheel (away from you as the buffing wheel rotates away from you) with medium light pressure.

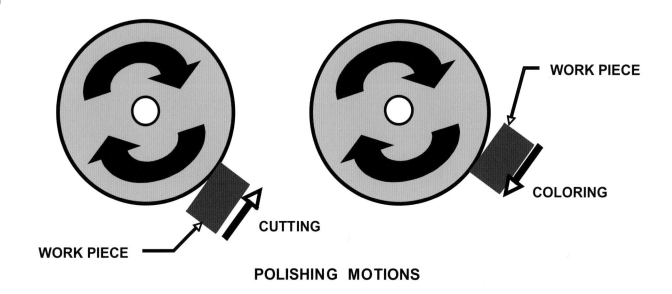

CUTTING

WORK PIECE

WORK PIECE

COLORING

POLISHING MOTIONS

When cutting a work piece to remove surface seams, scratches, or other irregularities, the work piece should be moved in the opposite direction of the buffing wheel. This is typically done by pulling the work piece toward you as the buffing wheel is rotating away from you. Cutting should be done until the surface is uniform in appearance. When buffing to bring out the color of the work piece, it should be moved in the same direction as the rotating buffing wheel, using slightly less pressure to avoid burning the work piece. This is done using various buffing wheels and compounds until the desired finish is obtained.

BUFFING WHEEL AND COMPOUND REFERENCE

Material	Rough Cut		Final Cut/Initial Polish		Final Polish	
	Wheel	Compound	Wheel	Compound	Wheel	Compound
Stainless Steel	Sisal	Emery	Spiral Sewn	Stainless Steel	Loose	Stainless Steel
Steel, Iron, and other Ferrous Metals	Sisal	Emery	Spiral Sewn	White Rouge	Loose	Jeweler's Rouge
Soft Metals (Aluminum, Copper, Brass, etc.)	Sisal	Emery	Spiral Sewn	Tripoli	Loose	White Rouge
Nickel and Chrome Plate	Not applicable		Spiral Sewn	White Rouge	Canton Flannel	Jeweler's Rouge
Silver and Gold	Not applicable		Not applicable		Canton Flannel	Jeweler's Rouge

Choosing the Correct Wheel and Compound

Before polishing a piece of metal, you must first determine if any cutting needs to be done, or if you can proceed directly to the coloring process. Although any polishing compound could be used on any buffing wheel, this would not be the most practical or economical approach.

For cutting, you should use a harder wheel, such as sisal or spiral sewn. With these wheels, you should use greaseless compound (in the appropriate grit for the amount of cutting to be done), emery, or stainless compounds.

For coloring, you should use a softer wheel, such as flap or loose cotton. Tripoli, jewelers' rouge, or white rouge should be used with these softer wheels to bring out the best color.

Buffing Speeds

Although most commercially available buffing motors are single speeds (around 3,600 rpm for those designed for home shop use), you do have some latitude for the surface speed of the buffing wheel itself. Surface speed is referred to as surface feet per minute (SFPM) and for best results, should be maintained between 3,600 and 7,500. Higher speeds will provide better and faster results, but you should work at a speed at which you feel comfortable. The formula for calculating SFPM is:

SFPM = 1/4 x buffing wheel diameter x rpm of buffer motor

For a buffer motor that runs at 3,600 rpm and a 4-inch wheel, the SFPM would be 3,600 rpm. Surface feet per minute for 6-, 8-, and 10-inch wheels would be 5,400, 7,200, and 9,000 rpm respectively.

Tips and Tricks

You should not use multiple compounds on any one wheel, as this will result in multiple grits on the same wheel, which will cause scratches rather than remove them. In other words, if you have used one sisal wheel with emery compound, and need to use a stainless or other compound, you should use a different wheel.

When applying compound to the buffing wheel, you should apply it for no more than a second. Then, use the work piece to work the compound onto the wheel. Trying to apply compound to the entire surface of the buffing wheel itself is wasteful of both time and material.

A method to remove swirl marks that come from hand sanding or polishing is to wet the part with a damp cloth, sprinkle on some talcum powder or cornstarch, and then buff until the swirls are gone.

Any time that you are working with rotating machinery, safety must be of primary concern. A buffing wheel has two distinct zones, the unsafe zone and the safe zone. The portion of the buffing (or grinding) wheel that is rotating toward you (or the work piece) is the unsafe zone. The portion of the buffing wheel that is rotating away from you is the safe zone. You should apply the work piece to the safe zone or area of the buffing wheel that is rotating away from you. If you apply the work piece to the buffing wheel in the unsafe zone (area moving toward you), the work piece could be thrown toward you if you lose your grip on it. This could inflict injury or death to you or others in the immediate area.

When buffing, you should always wear safety goggles or a face mask, heavy gloves, and a shop apron. Loose hair and/or clothing should be tied back, so as not to be accidentally caught up and wound around the rotating buffing wheel or shaft.

POLISHING

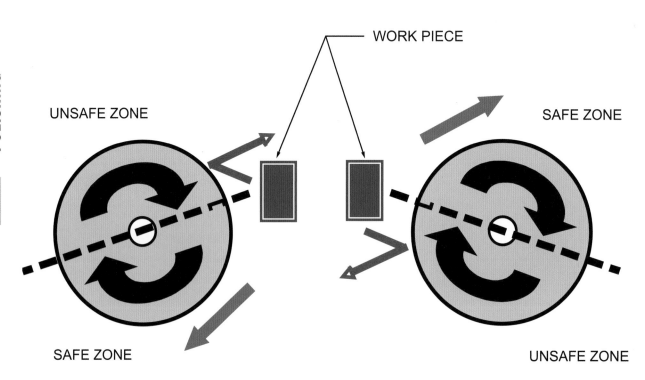

WORK PIECE

UNSAFE ZONE

SAFE ZONE

SAFE ZONE

UNSAFE ZONE

WORK PIECE IN RELATION TO BUFFING OR GRINDING WHEEL ROTATION

Whether you are grinding, cutting, or buffing, you must be aware of the potential for danger when introducing a work piece to a spinning wheel. The work piece should not contact the grinding or buffing wheel on any location where the wheel is rotating toward you. The work piece should only contact the rotating wheel in an area that is rotating away from you, so that if the work piece were to catch in the wheel, it would be pulled away from you rather than thrown at you.

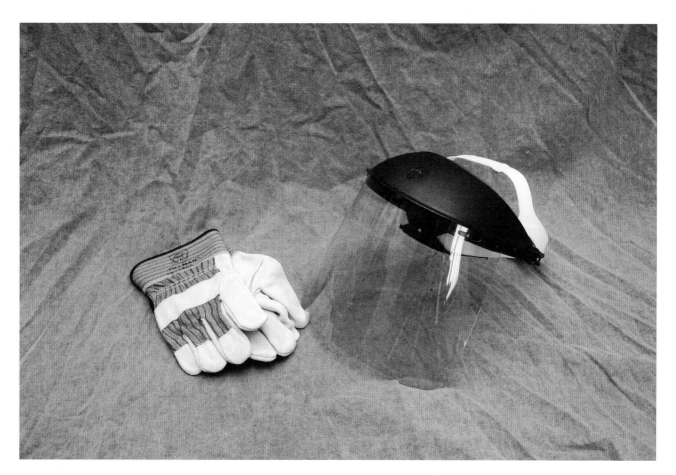

Whenever working with a grinder or buffer, you should always wear a pair of heavy work gloves, as either one of these tools will quickly remove skin if you should inadvertently contact the rotating wheel with your hand. You should also wear a full face shield as protection from excess compound. Although not shown, proper safety glasses are a good addition to the face shield.

CHAPTER 6
PLATING

Chrome plating has been around for a long time and is a great way to add some sparkle to your automotive project. For most classic cars and bikes, chrome bumpers and accents are standard fare. For hobbyists, adding chrome to high-profile areas like air cleaner covers, cylinder head covers, and exhaust pipes is the final touch to a superb ride. Enthusiasts can sometimes take it to extremes. For many, chrome is the ultimate finish, while for others, it is simply a place to start. Many different types of plating finishes are available, and if done properly and in the right amounts, serve as a great alternative or complement to chrome plating.

Plating Basics

Plating is a process of applying metal particles (chrome, tin, nickel, etc.) to a surface. To do this, electricity is used, so the correct term should be electroplating. By applying a positive electrical charge to the metal particles that are suspended in a liquid solution (allowing them to move), they can be attracted to an object that has been given a negative electrical charge.

Imagine connecting a cable from the negative side of a battery to the piece that is to be plated (the cathode). In similar fashion, a cable from the positive side of the battery is connected to a metal plate (the anode). With the cathode and anode both suspended in a plating solution (the electrolyte), positive ions from the anode flow through the solution and deposit the plating material onto the cathode.

Proper cleaning and surface preparation, accurate mixing of solutions, exact temperatures, and precise timing are critical to the success of any plating job. Like almost anything, practice combined with note taking allowing you to learn from your mistakes (and successes) will prove to be

Even though this blown hemi engine may look like a solid chunk of chrome with all of the sparkling accessories, most all of these components could be plated at home. Individually, all of these parts would fit into tanks that are smaller than 55-gallon drums. True, it would take quite a bit of time to plate all of these pieces, but your time is probably less expensive than the employees' time at a commercial plating shop.

invaluable as you learn to plate. With the vast array of plating kits available, and a large number of relatively small car or bike parts at your disposal, even hobbyists can plate their own parts.

Hobbyist-type plating kits are available from different sources. Metals to be plated will be of different chemical makeup and of different sizes. For these reasons, times and temperatures given in the following text for applying different types of plating should not be considered absolute. While they are recommendations from the sources for this book, it would be impossible to verify them with every manufacturer of the necessary products and processes. Use them as a guide, however, remembering you should always follow the directions included with the product you are actually using.

Safety Concerns

In addition to the labor-intensive nature of plating, another factor that contributes greatly to the expense are the costs associated with minimizing or eliminating harmful fumes that are present in large commercial plating operations. These fumes are minimal to nonexistent when plating is done on the hobbyist level. That is not to say that a commercial plater who isn't making money can suddenly declare himself a hobbyist to avoid being responsible for the fumes their business creates.

Fumes from nickel, copper, and zinc plating do not present any major health risk and are hardly noticeable. However, fumes emitted during chrome plating, degreasing, anodizing, and de-plating are unpleasant and dangerous. The chemicals used in all plating operations are toxic, and may cause blindness if they get into your eyes or burn if they make contact with your skin. You must remember that no matter what type of plating you are doing, certain safety precautions exist and must be followed to protect the health, safety, and general well-being of you and those around you. Any time that you are working around harmful chemicals, you should wear goggles, rubber gloves, and an apron over your regular clothes. Additionally, an exhaust fan and fume hood should be located in the area where the work will be taking place. For the hobbyist operation, a range hood such as those commonly found in residential kitchens works well. These are relatively inexpensive and can be purchased at home building supply stores.

You should always have a container of sodium bicarbonate (commonly known as baking soda) on hand to use in case of an acid spill. The baking soda should be sprinkled on the spill until the acid is neutralized. Then it should be mopped up and flushed with clean water.

Since plating chemicals contain heavy metals, they must not be flushed down the drain, no matter how small the quantity may be. Instead, you should evaporate as much water as possible from the tanks and then place the sludge at the bottom of the tank into a plastic container. It can then be disposed of by taking it to a chemical waste disposal station.

Setting Up a Home Plating Shop

If you are going to be doing plating on any sort of regular basis, you should consider doing some planning and setting up a portion of your garage or workshop specifically for this task. This is not to say that it has to be a permanent setup. However, some good planning toward efficiency, comfort, and productivity will enhance results in any workshop endeavor.

For best results of the various plating solutions and a comfortable working environment, the ambient room temperatures should be around 70 degrees Fahrenheit. The floor should be made of concrete, and for ease of cleanup, coated with epoxy. You should also have plenty of ventilation and access to running water.

Any shop requires adequate lighting, and more is always better than not enough. Fluorescent shop lights are available in several configurations suitable for commercial or hobbyist use. You will need to be able to inspect your work, so you must be able to see it clearly under good light.

Necessary Equipment

Most of the equipment required for doing your own plating is readily available and not very expensive. The following items can probably be found at Wal-Mart, Kmart, or other discount department stores: an aquarium thermometer, distilled water, rubber gloves, goggles, plastic apron, plastic-coated copper wire, wood or plastic stir sticks, acetone or lacquer thinner, plastic containers, baking soda, and a magnifying glass. You may need to go to a hardware, home building supply, or farm supply store for 18-gauge

For the bright nickel solution, Mike Boyle at Fat Catz Plating uses a square utility sink that has been modified to suit his needs. Nothing elaborate, but it works. Since this process creates some intense bubbling and foaming, additional boards are attached around the top edge to eliminate spillover.

For many of the processes, such as the bright acid copper solution, plastic 55-gallon drums are used. These are readily available at home supply centers and surplus outlets.

The original use of this tank is unknown, but it works well for Mike's chromic acid solution. The wide edge at the top is excellent for securing the copper tubing framework that is used for hanging parts.

bare copper wire, alligator clips, muriatic acid, a pH meter, sulfuric acid, 1/2-inch copper pipe, and a respirator with acid gas cartridges. For additional buffing and polishing equipment, refer to Chapter 5.

You won't need all of these items for all of your plating tasks, so you may choose to wait until you have acquired a particular plating kit to determine what is really needed for your particular application. You should also determine if you plan to start doing plating work for others or just for yourself. If you do plan on doing some work for others, you can begin writing off these start-up expenses as business expense, if the business pans out. You should also choose the quality of your newly purchased equipment accordingly.

Dry Side

Setting up a plating shop, whether at home as a hobbyist operation or as a business, requires two distinct areas: a dry side and a wet side. The dry side is where you will be grinding, sanding, and polishing pieces in preparation for plating. Additional room may be required for disassembly, reassembly, and product storage. Sanders and buffing wheels should be located as far away from the plating tanks as practical to avoid having dust and small metal particles spoiling your plating solutions. Having these items in a separate but adjoining room would be ideal. If you are forced to have this type of equipment in the immediate proximity of your plating tanks, you can place some sort of covers on your tanks and even hang a temporary curtain to help avert contaminating your plating solutions.

Having a workbench complete with a vise, various files, and all of the tools necessary for disassembly and reassembly will also be beneficial. Clean shop towels and storage for the necessary polishing compounds and related accessories are an added bonus.

Wet Side

The wet side is where the actual plating processes will take place. This area will be exposed to water, alkaline, and acid materials. Quite often, it will be a mess and may generate some less than pleasing smells. Cross-ventilation is a must, and an exhaust vent/fan should be a high priority when designing your plating area.

At Fat Catz Plating, all grinding, buffing, and polishing is done across the hall from the plating tanks. It is only a few steps away, yet far enough. It's in an enclosed room to keep all grinding material, buffing compound, and other contaminants away from the plating solutions. (The door was left open for this photo.)

The size of your plating tanks will have a direct impact on the size of the parts that you can plate. Most chopper parts and many parts used on hot rods are relatively small, making them ideal plating projects for the do-it-yourself plater. Whatever size tanks you decide you need, your workbench will need to be large enough to hold up to four of these tanks simultaneously and have sufficient room around the tanks for laying out parts.

If you choose to plate larger items, you can use plastic 55-gallon drums for your tanks. These would need to sit on the floor, rather than on a workbench. Larger tanks will allow you to plate larger parts, although they will require more chemicals and water to mix up the solutions. If you are going to be plating many parts of various sizes, a set of larger tanks will make good sense, but if you plan to just plate a few small items that would fit in a 5-gallon bucket, there is no need for a 55-gallon drum.

To make your plating process easier to keep clean, place the workbench adjacent to a sink. A step further would be to situate the workbench so that the surface naturally drains into the sink, allowing for quick and easy cleanup after plating is finished or in the event of a minor spill.

If you are planning to set up a permanent plating shop, you will most likely be required to construct a 2- or 3-inch-high step (dam) in the doorway to prevent liquid from a potential spill flowing into other parts of the building. To avoid problems from the beginning, you should check with your local building code enforcement officials to get their recommendations and requirements before you build.

Depending on the desired size of your workbench, discarded base cabinets with an appropriately sized countertop from a kitchen remodeling project, or even new, unfinished base cabinets from a home building supply store, would go a long way toward a suitable workbench.

You should use plywood or a Formica-type surface for the top, as particleboard or other similar building materials will quickly deteriorate when exposed to the types of liquids used when plating.

You must give the size (and weight) of the parts you are going to plate some thought before setting the height of your workbench. You may be able to plate small, lightweight parts in 5-gallon buckets sitting atop a typical kitchen-height countertop. However, larger, heavier parts require that the plating tanks be situated lower, so the parts can be easily placed in and removed from the tanks. One way to utilize a typical countertop is to recess the tanks into the countertop by cutting appropriately sized holes. When doing this, you must make sure that the holes are neither too close together nor too close to any countertop edges. You should also build a support beneath the tanks, as they can become quite heavy. Of course, any extra room in the base cabinets can be used for storage of extra plating supplies.

Heating the Solutions

It will be necessary to heat some of the solutions used in the plating process. An aquarium heater will be submersible, but may not completely fit into smaller plating tanks. In this case, the heater will need to be hung from the side of the tank. A simple way to do this is to simply loop a strand of plastic-coated wire around the neck of the heater and then crimp the end so that it fits over the edge of the tank.

To avoid breaking the glass tube in the heater, avoid bumping it with parts being placed into or pulled out of the tank. Also try to avoid adding water to the plating solution while the heater is hot, or placing a hot heater into a relatively cool solution. Having the heater completely submersed in the plating solution will minimize the possibility of cracking or breaking the glass when it is necessary to add water to the solution. Another method of protecting the heater is to slide a section of polynet tubing over it.

When setting the thermostat for the optimum temperature for your plating tank, set the adjustment at the midrange, then immerse it into the tank before the heater warms up. After an hour, check the temperature of the solution, and then adjust the heater accordingly. Check and adjust again as necessary after another hour until the heater is keeping the solution at the desired temperature.

You should not swap heaters from one tank to another, as small quantities of plating solution will be transferred into each tank. This plating solution from one process will contaminate the solution for the other process. The chrome plating solution is a rather aggressive step, so to avoid damage to the heater, the heater should be turned off and removed after the solution is adequately heated.

Another method of heating the plating solution is to pour or dip a portion of the solution into a ceramic-lined container and then heat the liquid on a hot plate or other similar heating device. Then carefully pour the heated solution back into the plating tank.

For solutions that require boiling, you can use a 110-volt ceramic heater. These will heat a solution to boiling quite rapidly, but they should not be used for situations requiring a specific temperature, as they usually have no thermostat.

A Suitable Power Source

To provide electric current for a small plating job, you have some affordable choices. These are a 25- or 60-amp rectifier, or a 6- or 12-volt battery. Any of these power sources will adequately plate surfaces of up to about 30 square inches. For occasional use, a battery will work. However, for regular use, one of the rectifiers would be a better choice. Rectifiers have a built-in rheostat, making the power easier to control, which will provide more consistent results. Larger rectifiers, such as those rated around 250 amps, will plate parts up to approximately 200 square inches in size, making this a suitable power source for the small production shop.

Most small plating jobs that could be done in a home shop require only 2 to 6 volts, making a 6-volt battery an ideal choice. A larger battery, such as a 12-volt car battery, can be used, but will provide too much voltage. To siphon off some of this excessive voltage, you can wire in one or multiple light sockets between the battery and the plating tank. By also wiring in a rheostat (or a dimmer switch), you can manually turn on or dim multiple lights to control the voltage. It would make sense to also wire a voltmeter in line to monitor the voltage to increase consistency in your plating results.

Chrome plating requires sufficient power to obtain satisfactory results. To supply adequate power for chroming parts up to about 200 square inches, you can combine a six-volt battery from a golf cart or deep cycle trolling motor with a battery charger. Draw the power from the battery, but keep the charger wired to the battery to keep it fully charged. If the chrome will still not "throw" (meaning deposit), you can wire additional batteries in parallel to provide additional amps.

Determining the proper power source will depend on the unique material and size of the work piece that is being plated, making hard-and-fast rules for each and every plating situation impossible to publish. However, knowing Ohm's Law will allow you to quickly determine what is necessary. Ohm's Law states "in an active electric circuit, the amperes are equal to the voltage divided by the resistance." In other words: A=V/R, V=AxR, or R=V/A, where V is voltage measured in volts, A is amperage measured in amps, and R is resistance measured in Ohms. By knowing any of the two measurements, you can easily determine the third.

Hanging the Parts

Although it may not seem like a big deal, how you actually hang the parts when plating is critical to the success of the plating. The wire used to hang the part in the plating solution is how the electrical current is carried to the part being plated, so the material of the wire is critical. Copper wire (10–20 gauge) is probably the most universally used wire for plating. Chrome plating requires high amperage, so you will need to use a heavier gauge (lower number) wire, or double up the wire. Brass wire does not oxidize as fast as copper wire, making it a better choice for hanging, although it is not as commonly available. Steel wire or copper-coated steel wire does not conduct properly, so you should avoid its use for hanging parts to be plated.

Wherever the hanging wire touches the part to be plated, a mark will be left where plating solution could not adequately cover the part. To avoid these marks, look for methods of attachment that will not affect the surface that will most commonly be seen. You can route the hanging wire through mounting holes where mounting screws will hide any marks. If there are no mounting holes, loop the hanging wire so that it touches only the edges of the work piece. Sometimes it will be possible to form the hanging

wire into a "hook" and hook the part from the back side. If you are careful, you can usually buff out wire marks.

To plate small screws and bolts, you can thread a portion of the fastener into a thin sheet of brass or copper, and dip the entire sheet into the plating solution. For plating just the heads of bolts or screws, you can also wrap a hanging wire around the threaded portion of the fastener and dunk just the portion to be plated.

When hanging parts, you should also be aware of hydrogen and air entrapment. All plating solutions form hydrogen bubbles, and when trapped or otherwise allowed to collect, these bubbles form a gas pocket that keeps the area

HANGING PARTS

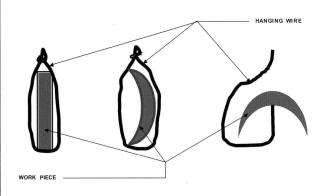

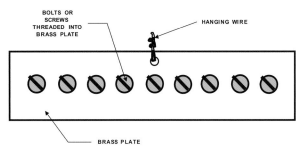

To achieve full coverage of the plating solution, you must be careful how you actually hang the parts. You will need to use wire that is soft enough to easily work with, yet stiff enough to hold the shape you need. The hanging wire should be situated so that it touches the least amount of the surface to be plated. This can be done by placing the wire where it touches only the edges of the work piece, as shown in the left and center examples. On some pieces, you may be able to bend the wire out, around, and underneath the part to be plated. Screws or bolts can be plated by threading them into a piece of brass sheet stock.

from plating. Work pieces that have concave surfaces, cylindrical objects, or angled objects are all susceptible to hydrogen bubbles being trapped. Pieces should be situated in the plating tank with any concave surfaces up, so that bubbles can escape. With a concaved surface down, the bubbles would become trapped as they naturally try to float upward to the surface. Cylinders should be situated in the plating tank in a vertical orientation, rather than horizontal, for the same reason. Angled material or brackets should also be positioned in the tank in such a way that hydrogen bubbles cannot become trapped.

Chrome Plating

How It's Done

One of the first things that must be determined prior to plating is what the piece or part is actually made of. The person doing the plating needs to know this so the part can be prepped properly. Aluminum, steel, brass, die cast, or pot metal can all be plated, but they each require different steps in preparation. No matter what the material, it must be clean and free of any corrosion, paint, or other plating of any kind. To eliminate any of these, the piece to be plated is usually washed in an acidic solution. However, some materials will not survive the normal acidic solution bath, and therefore must be media blasted first, and then followed up with a bath in a much milder acidic solution. Knowing what type of material you are dealing with obviously becomes important, as you don't want a one-of-a-kind trinket that will be the finishing touch for your project to simply melt away in the acid bath when it should have been media blasted.

After stripping the piece down to its bare bones, you can see any flaws (structural or cosmetic) that need to be addressed prior to plating. Before actually making any repairs or alterations, however, the metal needs to be sealed by applying a strike coat of hard copper plating. Like applying sealer between the primer and the color coats when painting, this hard copper strike coat seals the underlying metal in place and keeps any imperfections from working their way into the surface finish. You must realize, however, that when you are making a part that will be plated, it needs to be as straight and smooth as possible before going to the plating shop. Most plating shops are essentially in the business of repairing or refinishing, and generally not interested in fabricating (or refabricating) inferior parts or sloppy workmanship.

Methods used to repair imperfections such as dents, pits, or cracks vary, depending on their size and the material that needs to be repaired. To remove dents in most materials, a combination of grinding and hammering is used. Although a dent is typically thought of as a low spot that must be hammered out from the back, the material being pushed in when the dent is formed usually results in a high spot somewhere else. This high spot will need to be hammered inward or ground down. Holes, cracks, or pits are usually repaired by welding. The actual type of welding and the material used will greatly depend on the material being repaired. For books providing additional information on welding and metallurgy, check out www.motorbooks.com. Unlike when prepping for paint, plastic body filler can not and must not be used when prepping pieces for chrome or any other type of plating. A relatively new paint product that looks very convincingly like chrome and allows the use of plastic body filler is discussed later in this chapter.

When the part to be plated has been returned to the correct shape (if necessary), it will be sanded and polished before it is coated with acid copper plating. Small pits or other minute imperfections are filled in with this acid copper plating, much like high-build primer is used to fill similar surface imperfections prior to paint. Just as the paint's primer on the high spots is sanded off, excess copper is removed by additional polishing. This application of copper and polishing process is repeated until all of the imperfections have been removed.

Once all possible imperfections are removed during the acid copper plating process, the piece is dipped into a vat to receive a coating of nickel plating. Should any imperfections be found at this point, the part is polished again and coated with copper plating once more before receiving another coating of nickel plating. Although this process can be repeated as often as necessary, it becomes very labor intensive, so it is best to remove all of the imperfections as early in the game as possible. Only after all of the imperfections have been eliminated is the part ready to be chrome plated.

Much like when painting, surface preparation is the most important and time-consuming step. With all of this

AIR ENTRAPMENT

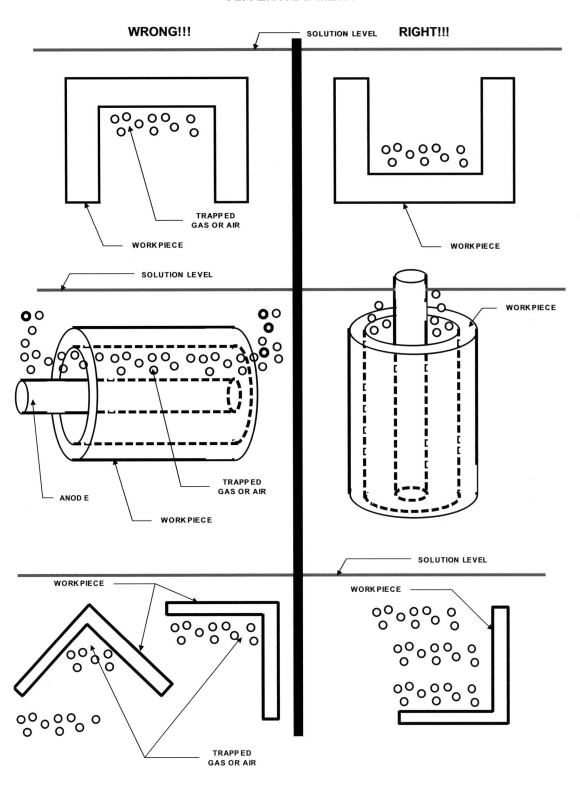

The more shapely that a particular work piece is, the more susceptible it is to hydrogen and air entrapment. Parts should be hung in the plating tank so that hydrogen is allowed to escape from the part, rather than be trapped by it. This is especially important in work pieces that are composed of angles or formed from any sort of tube (round, square, hex, etc.).

Contrary to popular belief, most of the work that goes into chrome plating is surface preparation. Other than routine applications of chrome polish whenever you wash your chopper, everything else is done prior to the relatively short dip into the chrome tank.

surface preparation completed, the chrome finish is achieved by dipping the nickel-plated part into a vat of chrome solution. A tank filled with chrome solution is equipped with wiring and an energy source, so that when a low-voltage current is applied, the chrome solution is attracted to the part to be plated. After submersion into the chrome solution for the correct amount of time, the plated part receives a water bath. This water bath does two things: it neutralizes the chrome solution and washes off excess solution. If done properly, this freshly plated part will have that brilliant, shiny finish that attracted us to chrome in the first place.

If the plating appears too thin, it was not left in the chrome solution long enough. If the plating is discolored, it was most likely left in the chrome tank too long, acquiring an excessive buildup. Should either of these situations arise or if imperfections are found, the part must be stripped and the entire process repeated, so take great care to do it right the first time.

Copper Plating

Copper plating is commonly used as a "primer" beneath nickel, tin, solder, or chrome plating, or it can be used as a decorative surface finish on its own. Copper plating can be applied to lead, pewter, brass, pot metal, steel, zinc, tin, copper, and aluminum that has been treated with zinc to aid in the adhesion of the final plating to the substrate.

When used as a substrate to other surface finishes, cyanide copper has been used extensively in the past as a strike coat. As people become more concerned for their personal health and safety in the workplace, cyanide is becoming less common, being replaced with flash copper.

Flash Copper

This more user-friendly version of copper plating is a great method of increasing adhesion between acid copper, nickel, or chrome plating to the material being plated. In addition to the obvious benefit of not containing cyanide, the use of flash copper also results in more uniform coverage. A finer grain of flash copper also improves corrosion resistance.

Prior to plating, immerse the part to be plated in degreaser for approximately five minutes at 140 to 200 degrees Fahrenheit, and then rinse with a spray of distilled water. Depending on the material to be plated and the desired texture, you may need to media blast the surface. Degreasing should be done prior to media blasting to avoid pushing any grease or contaminants into the surface, but should also be done afterward, as well.

FLASH COPPER PLATING APPLICATION TABLE

Time	Application	Plate Thickness
15 minutes	As a primer for other surface finishes over lead, zinc, or pot metal	0.00025 inch
30 minutes	As a primer for other surface finishes over steel	0.00050 inch
60 minutes	When used as the final finish	0.00100 inch

After applying the flash copper, buff and polish the surface with white buffing compound. It can then be plated with nickel and finally chrome for the common triple chrome plating, or simply with nickel, for a less shiny but still attractive surface.

If you choose copper as your final surface finish, you can build the surface thickness by adding acid copper. To help prevent discoloration to the copper surface, apply a coat or two of clear lacquer (if available) or metal wax designed for copper finishes.

PLATING

FLASH COPPER PLATING TROUBLESHOOTING TABLE

Problem	Cause	Remedy
Plating peels off or is discolored	Poor preparation or inadequate surface cleaning	Improve cleaning and rinsing procedures
Pitted plating (orange peel appearance)	Impurities in plating solution	Clean pump filter
Rough plating	Amperage set too high	Reduce current
Dark deposits	Zinc, lead, or iron contamination	Improve rinsing between acid pickling and plating
Dull appearance of plating	Insufficient buffing	Buff and repolish
Plating peels off	Surface heat created when buffing	Reduce pressure on buffing wheel

Bright Acid Copper

Acid copper can be used for the same purposes of flash copper, but its use is intended more for rough, irregular surfaces. Much as high-build filler primer is used over extensive bodywork or other rough surfaces when prepping for paint, acid copper can be built up with several coats. Use wet or dry sandpaper between applications of acid copper to obtain a smooth surface. For a higher-quality finish, buff each layer of copper prior to adding another coat.

Typical plating time for acid copper is 15 to 20 minutes, but an object may be left in longer to obtain a heavier layer. However, if left alone too long without agitation, coral-like growths that are difficult to remove will form on the part. Reducing the current and slight agitation of the part during the plating process will help to minimize these growths. For a finer finish, the tank temperature should be increased, while the amperage is reduced.

Prior to acid copper plating, degrease the part to be plated by immersing in degreaser for approximately five minutes at 140 to 200 degrees Fahrenheit, then rinse with a spray of distilled water. Use a nylon abrasive wheel or a media blast, and buff and polish to obtain the desired surface

Bright acid copper is used to fill low spots. When finished with this step, an acid-copper-plated part should be void of any low spots. Any imperfections can be removed by polishing.

finish as necessary. Degrease a second time if the part has been buffed and polished. If you are applying acid copper directly over a coating of flash copper, a thorough spray rinsing should be sufficient, rather than degreasing.

Thickness of acid copper plating is dependent directly on the amount of time in the tank and the amperage of the solution in the tank. Practice and experience is more critical in this form of plating than in others, as the operating range is fairly broad. Additional build can be achieved by increasing the amperage. However, if you are not careful, you will end up with dark brown plating that will easily wipe off.

ACID COPPER PLATING APPLICATION TABLE

Time	Plate Thickness
15 minutes	0.00025 inch to 0.00050 inch
30 minutes	0.00050 inch to 0.00100 inch
60 minutes or longer	0.00100 inch plus

After applying the acid copper, buff and polish the surface with white buffing compound. Then it can be finished with nickel plating or a layer of chrome added for a triple chrome-plated part.

Nickel plating is similar to the base coat of a base coat/clear coat paint system in that it provides the mirror image that is typically associated with chrome plating. The chrome plating is similar to the clear paint over a base paint color, as it provides the shine and gloss. Nickel plating by itself has a slight gold tint to it.

ACID COPPER PLATING TROUBLESHOOTING TABLE		
Problem	Cause	Remedy
Plating peels off or is discolored	Poor preparation or inadequate surface cleaning, or Surface heat created when buffing	Improve cleaning and rinsing procedures, or Reduce pressure on buffing wheel
Pitted plating (orange peel appearance)	Impurities in plating solution	Filter solution through activated charcoal
Rough plating	Amperage set too high	Reduce current
Dark deposits	Zinc, lead, or iron contamination	Improve rinsing between acid pickling and plating
Dull appearance of plating	Insufficient buffing	Buff and repolish

Nickel Plating

Nickel plating is one of the plating processes used in "triple chrome" plated parts, but it can be suitable as a finish all its own. Although it is often used as part of the chrome plating process, when used by itself, nickel has a duller or flatter look, almost like lead. Nickel plating can be "shined up" a bit with chrome polish, but if you desire a shiny finish, you should go ahead and chrome the part in question.6-96-10

Before applying a nickel plate to a surface, you must first obtain the desired surface texture. If you are looking for a mirrorlike finish, you will need to buff and polish the part. For more of a flat or dull appearance, bead blasting the part beforehand will be in order. To obtain a brushed appearance, buff the part with a nylon abrasive wheel. For cleaning the part prior to plating, immerse the part to be plated in degreaser for approximately five minutes at 140 to 200 degrees Fahrenheit and rinse with a spray of distilled water.

The use of the nickel-plated part will determine the recommended plate thickness, which, in turn, will determine the amount of time required for the part to be immersed in the nickel plating tank. The following chart gives recommendations for time, application, and plate thickness.

After plating, buff the plated part with white buffing compound and a spiral-sewn wheel to enhance the finish. To remove grease left over from buffing, soak the nickel-plated part in hot degreaser.

NICKEL PLATING APPLICATION TABLE		
Time	Application	Plate Thickness
15 minutes	Indoor or decorative items	0.00025 inch
30 minutes	Nuts and bolts, brackets, hand tools, guns	0.00050 inch
60 minutes	Motorcycle, automotive, or outdoor fittings	0.00100 inch

The engraved air cleaner and exhausts on this chopper have been nickel coated. Note how they have a slightly gold or yellowish cast to them.

NICKEL PLATING TROUBLESHOOTING TABLE

Problem	Cause	Remedy
Plating peels off	Poor preparation or inadequate surface cleaning	Acid etch or sand blast part, verify that degreaser is mixed properly
Pitted plating (orange peel appearance)	Impurities in plating solution	Add 1–3 teaspoons of hydrogen peroxide per 2 gallons of nickel solution
Rough plating	Amperage set too high	Reduce current by 1 amp per 15 square inches of surface area being plated
Rough plating, black streaks, or dark deposits	pH too high or low	Adjust pH to 3.5–4.5
Bright plating on high areas only or dull appearance of plating	Insufficient brightener in solution	Add brightener
Bright plating except in very low areas	Excessive brightener	Remove brightener by filtering

Chrome Paint as an Alternative

If you really desire to have the look of chrome, but the part is made of some material that cannot be chromed, or you can't fit the part in the chrome tank, or you just don't feel comfortable around electricity and liquids at the same time, you can still have that chrome look. Alsa Corporation manufactures MirraChrome, a paint product that is virtually impossible to distinguish from traditional chrome plating. MirraChrome is an acetone/alcohol-based coating that will provide a mirrorlike reflection that is 95 to 98 percent that of traditional chrome plating when applied over a glass-smooth surface. In other words, it will look just a bit darker when compared to chrome.

If you can paint, you can use this product, as its application is straightforward. While the product itself may seem pricey, it is comparable to the price you would pay to have a professional shop chrome plate your pieces. A great

benefit of MirraChrome is that it can be used on metal, plastic, fiberglass, and body filler. This feature alone allows this product to be used in many applications and for many parts that cannot be chrome plated. Except for the tires, you could essentially have your entire chopper or hot rod appear to be chrome plated, if you so desired.

After surface preparation and cleaning, the surface to be painted chrome should receive a coat of black base coat. Then spray a coat of clear with the appropriate hardener (Alsa Corporation recommends their Alsa Speed Clear mixed 4:1 with their Alsa Speed Hardener). For the best results, Alsa recommends waiting 10 days to make sure that the clear has fully cured, then wet sand and buff. Next, clean the surface with alcohol or an alcohol/water mixture and dry, making sure the dry surface is streak-free. Mirra-

The darker appearance of the painted chrome is very apparent when compared to the other parts that are either chrome plated or polished. A great benefit of chrome paint is that it can be applied to surfaces that cannot be chrome plated, such as plastic filler or fiberglass parts.

Granted, this rear fender looks dark, because it is reflecting the ceiling from high above, but if you look at the vertical portions of the fender, you will note that it looks darker than normal chrome. This is a tip-off that the surface is painted chrome rather than chrome plating.

Chrome is then applied in very light coats until the desired look is achieved. Now, wait for at least 48 hours for all of the solvent to evaporate. Remove overspray from the surface with a very soft, lint-free cloth. This step will greatly improve the final appearance. Finish the task by applying another coat of clear, allow to fully cure, then sand and buff as desired.

Other Metal Finishes

Metal finishes are limited only by your imagination. A popular finish is to work the metal to perfection by hammering, grinding, and sanding. Then, to prevent the quick formation of rust or other corrosion, the metal must be protected by applying either clear paint or powder coat. Some other metal finishes are listed below.

Black Chrome

This surface finish can range from a matte finish to a brilliant shine, depending on the amount of polishing done before and after the application of black chrome. Common examples of matte finishes are cameras, binoculars, and other optical products. Glossier examples include high-end plumbing fixtures, trophies, and furniture. The substrate to which the black chrome is applied will have a distinct effect on the final surface appearance. When applied to a nickel-plated piece, the black chrome will take on a smoky appearance, while it will appear as a deeper black when applied to copper.

Bead blasting the part prior to plating will provide a matte finish. Buffing and polishing prior to plating will increase the luster of the finished piece.

Brushed Aluminum

Aluminum is so workable, it is very easy to manufacture a wide variety of spacers, brackets, or other items from this material. Even if you don't use a milling machine, aluminum can be whittled, ground, or sliced into usable parts. To improve upon the looks of the finished piece or to achieve the look of "poor man's billet," rub the surface with a Scotch-Brite pad. This will scuff up the surface, hiding minor scratches, and will give the look of a milled piece. To protect the surface, a layer of clear can be added by painting or powder coating.

Painted Aluminum

Aluminum can be painted, although proper preparation is essential to keep the paint on the surface. The surface can be rough, scuffed, or buffed to provide the desired texture, but then it should be coated with an etching primer such as PPG's DPLF epoxy primer. After application of the etching primer, paint can be applied.

Antique Finishes

Brass and tin plating have been around for a long time and as such have stood the test of time. For a nostalgic appearance, either of these two finishes would be appropriate. Depending on the surface preparation, they can be made to look old and worn, or like brand-new, whichever you prefer.

Brass Plating

Brass plating can be applied to steel or other surfaces that have received a coating of bright nickel. To achieve an antique brass finish, the surface can first be allowed to oxidize and then plated with brass. For the shiniest brass finish, such as on band instruments, plumbing fixtures, or the foot rail at your favorite drinking establishment, the work piece should first be buffed to the highest gloss possible and then plated.

Copper Coloring

Copper plating can be used for antique-appearing finishes. However, if copper is left untreated or unprotected, it will quickly begin to darken. Copper can also be colored by applying heat from a propane torch or other comparable heat source. The torch is held close to the surface until the copper begins to change colors. When the copper part has cooled, it can be buffed to the desired gloss. After buffing the copper or to stop the natural oxidizing process, two or three coats of clear paint should be applied, with the copper further protected by a coat of paste wax.

Tin Plating

Tin plating can generally be applied directly over copper, steel, brass, and bronze. To apply tin plating over pot metal, it may be necessary to first apply a coating of flash copper. Tin plate is typically used for food handling equipment or utensils, due to its nontoxic qualities, but is also ideal for electrical connections, due to its excellent soldering capabilities.

Before applying tin plate to a surface, you will need to buff and polish the part, if you are looking for a mirror-like finish. To achieve a flat or satin appearance, the part to be tin plated should be cleaned with a nylon abrasive wheel or bead blasted. For cleaning the part prior to plating, immerse it in degreaser for approximately five minutes at 140 to 200 degrees Fahrenheit, and rinse with a spray of distilled water. The tin solution requires tin anodes, tin concentrate, distilled water, and battery acid.

PLATING

In fine military fashion on this tribute chopper, several items have been brass plated. The foot pegs have been brass plated over a coating of bright nickel. For a highly polished surface, the bright nickel coating would need to be polished prior to receiving the brass plating.

This chopper is unique in that all of the sheetmetal surfaces are constructed from copper sheet stock that has been cut and welded as necessary. Then the copper has been colored by heat.

A closer look at the rear fender gives a better look at the coloring effect. As heat is applied to the copper surface, the copper will change colors, depending on the amount of heat that is absorbed into the material. This can be done lightly or heavily to achieve different patterns of color. When finished coloring, the copper must be protected with clear powder coat or clear paint to prevent additional oxidation from diminishing the effect.

Mike Boyle at Fat Catz Plating demonstrated the chrome plating process on a transmission cover. Mike claims that his process differs from that used by some shops, but it works well for him. Since Fat Catz Plating is a one-man operation, Mike knows what works and what doesn't, as he does all the work on his customers' pieces.

This stock painted transmission cover is what Mike started with for this demonstration. A nice-looking piece, but rather bland.

To remove the factory paint, Mike will utilize his media blasting cabinet. For a relatively small piece such as this, he could sand the paint off by hand or use paint stripper, but bead blasting will be much quicker for removing the epoxy paint.

PLATING

Looking through the observation window, we can see the difference between the area that has been blasted and the area where the painted surface still needs to be removed. All blast cabinets will have an observation window. Although it would be a minor detail in the selection of a blasting cabinet, you should consider the positioning of the window before you buy.

With the paint removed, Mike now uses a belt sander to smooth the surface completely. This is where any casting marks or scratches would be removed. Although he isn't using a full face mask, note the use of gloves, respirator, safety glasses, and a heavy hooded shirt for protection.

To polish the surface prior to plating, Mike polishes the transmission cover, using Turkish gray emery compound.

To apply tubed compound to the buffing wheel, peel back the cardboard slightly, then apply the surface of the compound to the wheel for just a moment. Using too much compound will simply be a waste of material.

After the work piece has been polished, the remaining buffing compound, wax, and oils must be removed. The work piece is suspended from a metal wire and then submerged into a soap and degreaser solution.

A standard step at Fat Catz Plating, but not at all plating shops, is to scrub each piece with a soft brush while it is in the soap and degreaser solution.

This step of scrubbing the part with a soft brush revealed that the surface wasn't as smooth and free from defects as desired. Since Mike noticed this now, he can take the work piece back to the buffer to remove the irregularities, and then repeat all of the preceding steps to this point. If he doesn't remove the irregularities now, the finished work would not be right, and the entire procedure would have to be redone. Inspect your work!

Following the cleaning and degreasing step, the soap must be rinsed off with distilled water.

This is what the polished aluminum part looks like after being cleaned. At this point, it has simply had the epoxy paint removed by bead blasting and has been sanded, buffed, and cleaned. Not bad, huh? Still, it will get better.

Next, the work piece goes into an acid etch solution, which will help to ensure good adhesion of the following plating steps. After this step is a rinse tank that removes and neutralizes the etch solution, so it does not contaminate the next tank.

Before any aluminum parts can receive plating of any kind, they must first go into a Zincate solution. This step applies only to aluminum and not to other metals.

Next is the strike coat of hard copper, which acts as a filler and gives the work piece a pink look. This step is what eliminates the mostly outdated step of applying cyanide copper. More time in the tank will allow more copper to build on the surface if low spots need to be filled.

After rinsing the hard copper, the surface should be inspected and checked that all low spots are filled and that the surface is smooth. If low spots still exist, the work piece can go back into the hard copper.

The bright acid copper solution is much like the sealer in a paint system that keeps the strike coat copper filler separate from the nickel and chrome plating that will follow. All surface imperfections need to be removed by this point.

Coming out of bright acid copper, the work piece should be ready for the nickel- and chrome-plating process. If there are any imperfections, you should go back and fix them now and then repeat the preceding steps.

This is what bright acid copper looks like after polishing. If desired, the plating can be stopped at this point for a copper-plated work piece. However, the piece would need to be polished daily to retain this copper look. If not, it will quickly tarnish and eventually turn black. Other than daily polishing, clear-coat paint or clear powder coating can be applied.

Coming out of the bright nickel tank, notice how the work piece has a "whiter" look to it than with just the copper. With the nickel coating, it still has a bit of a yellow or gold tint to it. For better protection, the nickel coating should be coated with clear paint or powder coating.

The next step after nickel coating would be a quick dip in the chrome-plating tank, where the blue tint that is common with chrome plating is achieved. This is what the finished part looks like in place.

CHAPTER 7
ANODIZING

What Is Anodizing?

Although paint can be applied to almost any material and almost any metal can be polished, anodizing is a process suited just to aluminum. What actually happens when a piece of aluminum is anodized may seem complicated, but in practice the process is fairly simple.

When a piece of aluminum is anodized, it is submersed in a weak sulfuric acid, which acts as an electrolyte. The aluminum part (anode) receives a positive charge, while a piece of lead (cathode) receives a negative charge. When power is applied to the setup, the aluminum part begins to oxidize or corrode. Aluminum does not rust, but it does

The exhaust pipes, air cleaner cover, and front forks have been anodized purple on this colorful chopper. Although it still looks good, notice how the anodized pieces don't exactly match the painted purple on the fenders and tank. Any time that you are going to attempt to mix paint to match anodizing or powder coating, you should have an extra sample piece anodized or coated for the paint mixer to match to.

An anodized piece doesn't have to be a bright color. Anodized aluminum can be almost any color you desire.

oxidize, much the way steel rusts. This oxidation becomes a coating that is extremely hard and abrasion resistant. For several industries, achieving this tough and durable surface is the only reason for anodizing aluminum, and therefore, the process stops there, with the aluminum retaining its original gray/silver color.

However, metallurgists found that with some types of anodizing, the oxidation is porous, but uniform. This porosity allows dyes to be applied to the aluminum, giving the distinctive colors that most people think of when they think of anodized aluminum. A great advantage of anodizing compared to other finishes is that the color actually becomes an integral part of the aluminum piece, which results in a finish that cannot and will not flake or peel off. The process is also quick, and therefore relatively inexpensive when compared to other labor-intensive finishes.

The anodizing process uses water-based chemicals that are environmentally friendly. Other than normal workshop safety precautions, anodizing presents no need for extraordinary efforts in terms of safety.

The process for anodizing is to first clean the parts, brighten or etch them to yield the desired surface finish, and then anodize, dye (if desired), seal, and give them a final rinse.

Surface Preparation

Prior to anodizing, aluminum pieces must be free from wax, grease, oils, or other contaminants. The parts to be anodized should first be washed with soap and water and then cleaned again with a grease-removing product such as Simple Green or wax and grease remover used for paint preparation.

This belt cover is the perfect item to have anodized, as anodizing gives the work piece a harder, more durable surface. The fact that it is black to match the bike is good, but the highlighted areas that were masked from anodizing provide a detailing touch.

Aluminum that is to be anodized can be prepped to yield a bright finish or a matte finish. To achieve a bright or glossy finish, a procedure known as bright dipping is performed. If desired, you can also polish the aluminum piece using a buffing wheel with tripoli compound. To achieve a matte or machined looking surface, acid etch the part.

Bright Dipping

This is a process of dipping aluminum work pieces into a bath composed mainly of phosphoric and nitric acid. This bath levels the microscopic valleys and peaks of the surface, bringing the surface into the same geometric plane, providing a brighter finish.

Acid Etching

Washing the aluminum work piece in sodium hydroxide prior to anodizing will provide a matte finish. Corrosion or oxidation will occur rapidly, so the work piece must be anodized immediately to maintain the uniform satin appearance.

Anodizing

Even though there are different methods of anodizing, the most common method today uses sulfuric acid. The solution is typically around 15–25 percent, with an electrical current between 18 and 24 volts, and heated to around 70 degrees Fahrenheit for 10 minutes to 1 hour.

Adding Color

Color can be added to anodized aluminum by one of four different procedures: organic dyeing, electrolytic coloring, integral coloring, and interference coloring. Some methods are more suitable to automotive applications, while others are more suitable for architectural or medical use.

Organic dyeing is done simply by immersing the freshly anodized work piece into a liquid solution that contains dissolved dye in the color of your choice. The porous surface of the anodized aluminum absorbs the dye, so color intensity depends largely on dye concentration and immersion time.

Electrolytic coloring is a two-step process in which the work piece is dipped into a bath composed of inorganic metal solution. Tin, cobalt, nickel, and copper are typically used in this bath solution. The color from the metal solution is deposited into the pores of the work piece when electric current is applied. The aluminum then takes on the color of the inorganic metal.

Integral coloring is a one-step process combining the surface hardening of the anodizing procedure with a coloring procedure. Although the surface has more abrasion resistance than conventional anodizing, it is limited in color availability. This process is used extensively in architectural applications, such as door and window trim.

Interference coloring modifies the structure of the oxidation caused during the initial anodizing procedure. Metal is deposited more predominately at the base of the pores, making them more light fast, and therefore more resistant to potential damage caused by exposure to sunlight. Available colors range from blue to green and yellow to red. This is a relatively new process for adding color to aluminum.

Color Mixing

Commercially available anodizing dyes are transparent, which means you can overlap the colors. Although this will require some practice to determine timing and method, you could "fade" from one color to another easily if desired.

You can also mix dyes to achieve specific colors. This can be done by making one coloring solution with varying amounts of each color of dye. Doing this requires some forethought, or you may likely end up with a black

ANODIZING

or muddy-looking coloring. Or you could dip the work piece into separate tanks of the required colors until the desired color is achieved. This will require that you rinse the piece after each application of color, or the color from one tank will contaminate the color in another tank.

You can obtain a darker appearance by dipping the work piece into a tank of black dye after it has been dunked into a color tank and rinsed. Varying the time in the coloring tank will also affect the lightness/darkness of the color.

Color Application

Color is commonly applied by immersing the work piece into the coloring tank. This is probably the easiest method, but it is certainly not the only method. By using an airbrush, a paintbrush, an eyedropper, or a sponge, color can be applied to certain areas of the work piece. You could even color the inside of a part one color and the outside another color.

Masking

If you desire to allow the original color of the aluminum to show through in some areas, these areas can be masked off from color. This can be done by using masking tape, contact paper, or grease pencils. Masking tape or contact paper will need to be peeled off prior to the sealing process. Grease pencil will be removed during the heated sealing process.

Removing Dye

Should you need to remove color from a work piece, you can remove the color by soaking the work piece in household bleach. However, this must be done before the work piece has been sealed. After bleaching out the color, the work piece must be rinsed in room-temperature water. If the work piece is rinsed in hot water, the sealing process will begin, whether the color has been removed adequately or not.

The slightly candy-looking color is typical of aluminum parts that are anodized. Almost any color is attainable, and surface preparation can yield anything from a satin to a highly glossy surface.

Sealing

To protect the anodized surface from crazing or other color degradation, staining, or abrasion, the surface must be sealed. This closes the pores that were created in the original anodizing operation. Soak the part in boiling water or use one of the commercially available sealer products to lock in the color. After sealing, the part should be rinsed again, and then hung up to dry overnight.

Anodizing at Home

The following procedure is a bare-bones method of anodizing one or two pieces at a minimum expense, but will provide an overview of the process. If you choose to anodize parts on a regular basis, you should probably consult a source listed in the back of the book for more economical sources for sulfuric acid, dyes, and other supplies.

Necessary Equipment

To anodize at home, you will need a 6- to 12-volt battery charger, sulfuric acid, aluminum ground wire, and some aluminum foil. Additionally, you will need some sort of container that is large enough to completely immerse the work piece that you choose to anodize. You can find aluminum wire at an electronics store such as Radio Shack, and if aluminum foil is not already in your kitchen, it's as close as the grocery store.

To add color, you can use ordinary fabric dye found at a fabric store or discount store that sells material and other sewing supplies. These dyes are available in a variety of colors, but could also be mixed to achieve a custom color.

Safety Precautions

When mixing acid and water, you must remember to add the acid to the water, *never* the other way around. Add the acid slowly and stir gently to make sure that the two are mixed adequately. Be sure to wear goggles or a face mask to protect your eyes and rubber gloves to protect your hands.

When anodizing, the electricity running through the sulfuric acid solution creates hydrogen, which is extremely flammable. Do not smoke or have any other sources of ignition in the area. You should also ventilate the immediate area.

Sprinkle baking soda on any spilled sulfuric solution to neutralize the solution. When the spill quits fizzing, it has successfully been neutralized.

Setup

Determine what you are going to use for an anodizing tank. A rubber or plastic container will work best, as the sulfuric acid may eat through a metal tank. It will need to be large enough for the piece to be completely submerged without touching the bottom.

Use a piece of aluminum wire long enough to make a loop that is just slightly smaller than the bottom of your tank, and then run the wire up the side of the tank and out over the edge. Cover the looped section with aluminum foil. This loop will lie in the bottom of the tank and become the negative ground. Place the negative ground so that it lies flat in the bottom of the tank, if you haven't already done so.

Mix your solution of sulfuric acid in your tank so that the solution is between 15 and 25 percent. Remember to add the acid to the water, and not the other way around.

Anodizing Process

In addition to cleaning the parts with soap and water, 1 to 2 ounces of nitric acid in a gallon of distilled water will also serve as a good cleaning step to ensure even color. This should be done immediately before anodizing the part to keep unwanted oxidation to a minimum.

Connect the negative lead from the battery charger to the aluminum wire. Make sure the battery charger lead does not get into the anodizing solution. Connect the positive lead from the battery charger to an unobtrusive location on the part to be anodized, and then immerse the part in the solution. You will need to fashion some sort of hanging device to prevent the work piece from resting on the negative-ground aluminum foil located at the bottom of the tank. You should hang the work piece with aluminum wire so that the battery charger lead can be clipped to the hanging wire and kept out of the anodizing solution. Make sure that you do not allow the negative and positive leads from the battery charger to touch each other. Anodizing will require between 4 and 12 amps per square foot to be anodized, so set the battery charger accordingly. Turn the

BASIC ANODIZING SETUP

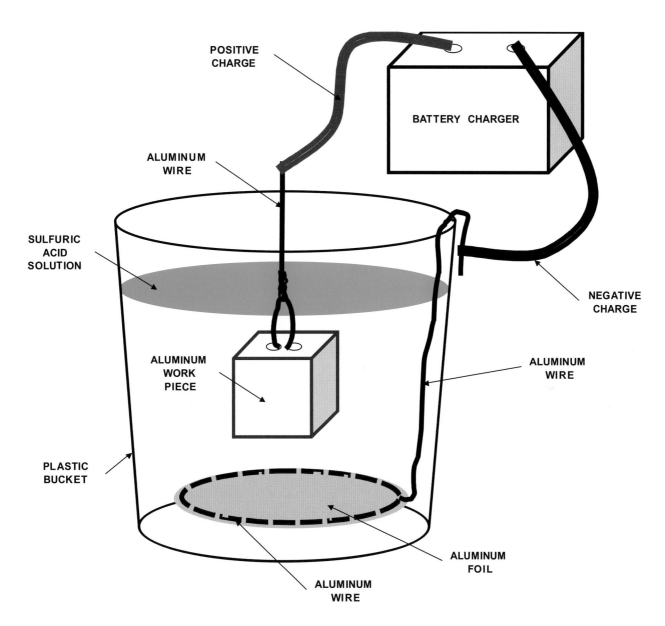

BASIC ANODIZING SETUP

This illustration shows a typical home anodizing setup. Sulfuric acid will eventually eat through metal containers, so you should use a plastic or rubber container. A commonly used tank for anodizing at home is a picnic cooler. These are readily available and easy to handle. They come in a variety of sizes, and they will hold most individual chopper parts suitable for anodizing.

charger on and watch for the work piece to begin to fizz (bubble around the edges).

After 10–15 minutes, small parts will most likely not be conducting any more electricity. Larger parts will require additional time. Turn the battery charger off, disconnect the part from the battery charger positive lead, and then rinse the part in cold water if you plan to add color. Rinsing the part in hot water will seal the part and prevent it from taking color. You should progress to the color step immediately to prevent an oxidation buildup between the anodizing and coloring steps.

Coloring Process

You should already have your dye solution mixed and waiting in a container that can be heated and is large enough for the part to be immersed. Part of the color will leech out during the sealing process, so you should mix the dye fairly strong. The part can touch the bottom during the coloring process, although contact with the bottom of the coloring tank might prevent color from reaching that portion of the part.

Submerge the work piece into the coloring solution and apply low heat (about 140 degrees Fahrenheit) such as on a stovetop. If possible, turn the part frequently to achieve uniform color. Leave the part in the coloring tank until it is slightly darker than your desired final color. Now remove the part from the coloring tank and rinse with cold water. Seal it by placing it in a container of clean, boiling water for 20 minutes. Rinse again and let dry.

Cleaning Anodized Aluminum

Gentle soap, such as dishwashing liquid and warm water, should be used to clean anodized aluminum. Since the surface is so hard, you can use an abrasive cleaning sponge if necessary to clean the surface. However, you should avoid using acidic or alkaline cleaners or solvents, as they may destroy or stain the finish.

SOURCES

Alsa Corporation

2640 East 37th Street, Vernon, CA 90058

www.alsacorp.com

877-238-8280

Unique and progressive paint and coatings

Arch City Custom Bikes

1692 Larkin-Williams Road, Fenton, MO 63026

636-349-0004

Chopper fabrication and assembly

Caswell Inc.

7696 Route 31, Lyons, NY 14489

www.caswellplating.com

315-946-1213

Plating and polishing kits, tools, and accessories

Eastwood Company

263 Shoemaker Road, Pottstown, PA 19464

www.eastwoodco.com

800-343-9353

Specialty tools and equipment

Fat Catz Plating

814 Olive Road, Park Hills, MO 63601-8235

573-431-5082

Chrome and nickel plating

Karg's Hot Rod Service

6505 Walnut Valley Road, High Ridge, MO 63049

www.kargshotrodservice.com

636-677-3674

Custom hot rod and chopper fabrication, bodywork, and painting

Mayhem Custom Paint & Graphics

430 MacArthur Street, Washington, MO 63090

636-390-8811

Custom artwork

PPG Refinish Group

www.ppgrefinish.com

The Paint Store

2800 High Ridge Boulevard, High Ridge, MO 63049

636-677-1566

PPG paint products and supplies

INDEX

MOTORBOOKS WORKSHOP

The Best Tools for the Job.

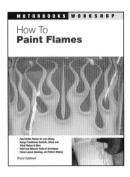

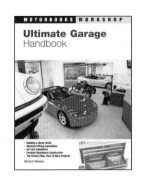

Performance Welding Handbook
2nd Edition
0-7603-2172-8 • 139436AP

How To Paint Flames
0-7603-1824-7 • 137414AP

**How To Build
Vintage Hot Rod V-8 Engines**
0-7603-2084-5 • 138703AP

**Honda & Acura
Performance Handbook**
2nd Edition
0-7603-1780-1 • 137410AP

**Hot Rod
Horsepower Handbook**
0-7603-1814-X • 137220AP

**How To Build the Cars of
*The Fast and the Furious***
0-7603-2077-2 • 138696AP

**How To Tune and Modify Engine
Management Systems**
0-7603-1582-5 • 136272AP

**Corvette Performance
Projects 1968–1982**
0-7603-1754-2 • 137230AP

Custom Pickup Handbook
0-7603-2180-9 • 139348AP

**Circle Track Chassis
& Suspension Handbook**
0-7603-1859-X • 138626AP

**How To Build A West Coast
Chopper Kit Bike**
0-7603-1872-7 • 137253

**101 Harley-Davidson Twin-Cam
Performance Projects**
0-7603-1639-2 • 136265AP

**101 Harley-Davidson
Performance Projects**
0-7603-0370-3 • 127165AP

**How To Custom Paint
Your Motorcycle**
0-7603-2033-0 • 138639AP

**101 Sportbike
Performance Projects**
0-7603-1331-8 • 135742AP

**Motorcycle Fuel
Injection Handbook**
0-7603-1635-X • 136172AP

**ATV Projects: Get the Most Out
of Your All-Terrain Vehicle**
0-7603-2058-6 • 138677AP

**Four Wheeler
Chassis & Suspension Handbook**
0-7603-1815-8 • 137235

**Ultimate Boat
Maintenance Projects**
0-7603-1696-1 • 137240AP

**Motocross & Off-Road
Performance Handbook**
3rd Edition
0-7603-1975-8 • 137408AP

**How To Restore Your
Wooden Runabout**
0-7603-1100-5 • 135107AP

Ultimate Garage Handbook
0-7603-1640-6 • 137389AP

**How To Restore John Deere
Two-Cylinder Tractors**
0-7603-0979-5 • 134861AP

**How To Restore Your Farm
Tractor**
2nd Edition
0-7603-1782-8 • 137246AP

**Mustang 5.0
Performance Projects**
0-7603-1545-0 • 137245AP

Visit **WWW.MOTORBOOKS.COM** or call 800-826-6600